Charles E Brimblecom

An Archer with Columbus

Charles E Brimblecom

An Archer with Columbus

ISBN/EAN: 9783743324480

Manufactured in Europe, USA, Canada, Australia, Japa

Cover: Foto ©ninafisch / pixelio.de

Manufactured and distributed by brebook publishing software (www.brebook.com)

Charles E Brimblecom

An Archer with Columbus

AN ARCHER WITH COLUMBUS

BY

CHARLES E. BRIMBLECOM

ILLUSTRATED

BOSTON
JOSEPH KNIGHT COMPANY
1894

An Archer with Columbus

by Charles E. Brimblecom

Illustrated

AD 1893

Joseph Knight Company
BOSTON

Chapter		Page
I.	THE WORLD IS ROUND	1
II.	FELIX WINS THE CROSSBOW	21
III.	A ROYAL MESSENGER	42
IV.	THE MONK'S GHOST	62
V.	THE PURSUIT	81
VI.	THE SAILING OF THE FLEET	106
VII.	THE NEW WORLD	128
VIII.	THE RETURN TO SPAIN	159

CHAPTER I.

THE WORLD IS ROUND.

ONE fine afternoon in the autumn of 1491, Ignacio Diaz, a tailor of the seaport town of Palos, was seated upon his table busily at work on a new cassock evidently intended for a priest or monk.

Diaz was a short, obese man with a round, red face. He was ignorant and avaricious, servile to his superiors and tyrannical to those beneath him. One of the chief victims of his petty tyranny was his apprentice, Felix Madrigal, a friendless orphan boy, whose unwilling drudgery was repaid with scanty fare and abundant blows.

Yet Ignacio Diaz considered himself a person of consequence; and after the events related in this story, his self-importance increased greatly, and for the rest of his life he boasted of the part he had taken in one of the grandest achievements in the history of mankind.

On that pleasant afternoon there was

a stranger seated in the little shop, — a man of dark complexion, with sharp, black eyes. His doublet was of green velvet, and he wore a long cloak of fine cloth. A broad hat with a plume shaded his face and a sword was buckled at his side.

After listening to the tailor's gossip for a while, the visitor suddenly asked, —

"Hast thou seen many strangers in thy town of late?"

"Strangers!" cried the tailor. "No, Señor, we see few strangers here. If you wish to see life, and bustling scenes, and magnificent costumes, — some of which I made myself, Señor, — you should go to Granada, where our mighty sovereigns, Ferdinand and Isabella, are besieging the infidel Moors. Heaven grant them success! No doubt you have seen service, Señor?"

To this question, which seemed to ask more than the mere words implied, the stranger replied shortly, —

"True! there *is* no doubt of it. What art thou staring at me for?"

This rude question was addressed to Felix Madrigal, the apprentice, who was neglecting his work and listening open-mouthed to the conversation.

"Sirrah!" cried the tailor to Felix, "have I not reproved thee a thousand times for thy impertinent curiosity? Attend to thy work, or —" And after fixing what was intended to be an awe-inspiring look upon the boy for the space of a minute, he slowly withdrew his eyes and again turned to the cavalier.

"I venture to suppose that you are connected with the custom-house," he said, in a wheedling tone. "An inspector, perhaps. Is it not so?"

"Suppose whatever pleases thee," answered the stranger, coolly. "Here, boy," he continued, tossing a coin to Felix, "thou wast reproved unjustly."

The tailor's red face grew redder at this rebuke. He folded up the cassock, which he had just finished, and said to Felix, harshly, —

"Here, jackanapes, take this cassock to Father Juan Perez at the convent of La Rabida, and bring back with thee his old one, which he wishes repaired. Hasten back. If thou delayest on the road, the yardstick shall dance o'er thy shoulders."

Felix sprang from his table at once, and having bound his ragged sash about his waist, and donned his little Andalusian hat, he took the bundle and gladly set out upon the sandy road leading to the convent, which he could see on a hill about a mile away.

The landscape was fresh and beautiful.

The northwest wind had brought welcome clouds from the distant mountains, and abundant rains had refreshed the thirsty soil. The broad vineyards, and orchards of figs and olives, seemed to smile and rejoice in the pure, delicious air. Far to the south and west shone the blue waters of the sea.

As Felix climbed the hill, he saw a caravel entering the mouth of the Tinto, and watched it as it glided up the river like a white swan. He recognized it as the *Pinta*, one of the fastest vessels on the coast, belonging to Señor Gomez Rascon of Palos.

He sat down on a rock by the wayside and gazed with intense enjoyment on the scene; but suddenly remembering the threat of his master, he sprang up and hastened on.

As he approached the convent of La Rabida, he saw a group of three persons at the gate. One was the porter, Lorenzo Tortosa, whom he knew well. Tortosa had been a crossbow man in the army of Ferdinand and Isabella; but having been severely wounded at the siege of Malaga, four years before, he had left the service and obtained a position as porter at the convent.

A tall man of noble and commanding appearance was addressing Tortosa. His snow-white hair and the deep lines of his face told of age and sorrow. In his hand he carried a large roll covered with a woolen cloth.

Beside him stood a pale, handsome boy of about the same age as Felix. The strangers seemed tired, and their clothing was worn and soiled with travel.

Felix stopped near the group and stared at them with curiosity. The porter seemed surprised, and the strange man repeated the request he had just made.—

"My son is hungry and thirsty. Can you give him a little bread and water to enable him to finish our journey?"

"Yes, Señor," replied the porter, very respectfully, "I was not sure I understood you."

At that moment a clear, authoritative voice called from the interior courtyard,—

"Who is there, Tortosa?"

The considerate porter, after  asking the strangers to excuse him for a moment, re-entered the gate to give his answer in a low tone.

Immediately Father Juan Perez, the Superior of the convent, appeared at the gate, and after courteously saluting the strange gentleman, invited him to enter.

He accepted the kind invitation of the priest, and passed through the gate, leading his boy by the hand. A fine young bloodhound, with black mouth and pendent ears, started up from the shadow of the wall and followed them.

Tortosa uttered a cry of alarm, and started forward to intercept him, but almost tumbled backward as the dog paused with a slight growl.

"Reverend Father!" cried Tortosa, "it is a dog! He may run mad at any moment. Will not the gentleman make him go out?"

"He is mine," said the strange boy, putting his arms about the dog's neck. "He will not harm any one unless I tell him to. Please let him come with me."

"Let the dog alone, Tortosa," replied Juan Perez, smiling. "Thou fearest a harmless animal more than a thousand fierce Moors."

The porter fell back uneasily and crossed himself, and the party went on.

Felix followed them as they traversed the cloisters and skirted the luxuriant garden of the convent. Here Juan Perez said to the boy, —

"Remain in the garden if you wish, my child, and one of the brothers will bring you refreshment." Then he passed into the building, followed by the gentleman.

The boy sat down on a bench under a fig-tree near the fountain; and presently a monk brought him bread and meat, and told him to pluck the purple figs above his head. He ate the food slowly and thoughtfully, sharing it with his dog.

After watching the young stranger for a little while, Felix slowly approached and spoke to him,—

"Good morning, Señor."

"How do you do, *cabálléro?*" responded the boy, in a low, pleasant voice. Felix was deeply astonished at receiving that distinguished title from the young stranger. Cavalier—gentleman! A feeling unknown before suddenly arose within him. Up to that moment he had regarded himself as an inferior being, a mere drudge and slave; but on being addressed by that courteous title, self-respect hitherto crushed down sprang up in his heart like a beautiful flower. Henceforth a new ambition was to inspire him. One kindly word turned him toward heroic heights. "Sit here beside me," continued the boy, smiling, "and let us talk together." And when Felix was seated, he asked, "What is your name?"

"Felix Madrigal. What is yours?"

"Diego Columbus," replied the boy.

"Where do you live?"

"We have no home," answered Diego calmly. "We came from Seville to this place."

"Is that your father that came with you?"

"Yes. My father is a sea captain."

"Did you walk all the way from Seville?"

"Yes, and it was beautiful in the mornings and evenings. My father tells me wonderful tales as we go along, so that I hardly ever feel tired."

"Why didn't you ride on mules?"

"We had but little money."

"Doesn't your father own a ship?"

"No. He has for a long time been engaged in greater affairs. He has been entreating the king and queen to give him ships in which he will sail across the ocean to the west until he reaches the Indies."

Felix looked puzzled. He had often heard the sailors of Palos speak of the Indies. He had also heard many tales of the terrible unknown ocean in the west.

"But the Indies are in the east," he cried.

"You can get there by sailing to the west, too. My father says so."

"Why, that's impossible," returned Felix, astonished. "That is the sea of darkness and dragons, and beyond is the end of the world. That's what all the sailors say."

"Oh, no. The world is round, and has no end, and — Oh, what a big cat! look at him! look at him!"

A huge black cat was standing in the

garden walk, arching his back and uttering low growls at sight of the dog. The bloodhound, unused to such defiance, suddenly darted forward in pursuit.

"Oh, stop him!" cried Felix, in a tone of fright.

"Here, Perrito! Perrito! back, back!" shouted Diego, springing up and running down the walk. But the cat had swiftly mounted the low wall of the garden, where he remained bristling and growling, and Perrito came back to his young master, who sharply rebuked him.

"Ah, little rogue," said Diego, as he returned, "thou must not touch the cat, or we shall banish thee."

"It is lucky that Father Juan Perez did not see your dog chase his cat," said Felix. "He values that beast more than anything else in the world, they say. He would have killed the dog, I dare say, and thrown you out of his gates."

"Then I will be very careful after this," said Diego, looking a little alarmed.

"What — what did you say about the world?" asked Felix, with some hesitation.

"Oh, I said the world is round like a ball. — Lie down, Perrito."

"Round!"

"Yes, my father has studied it and knows all about it. These are delicious figs."

"Is it possible!" cried Felix, amazed. "But how do the people on the under side stay on?"

"There is no under side. The world seems the same to them that it does to us."

"Astonishing! And are the king and queen going to give your father ships?"

"No, he has waited seven years; but their Highnesses are forever fighting the Moors, and cannot listen to us. Now, we are going to France to ask the French king to help us. If he refuses, we will go to the king of England, who wrote to my father and invited him to come. I read the letter myself."

"What! can you read?" asked Felix, with deep respect.

"Yes, of course. Can you not read?"

"N-o-o-o!" exclaimed Felix, as if Diego had asked him if he could fly. "How wise you must be. Ah, how I wish I could learn to read!"

"You *can* learn," replied Diego.

"Impossible!" said Felix gloomily.

While Diego was giving his companion more astonishing information about the world, Father Juan Perez appeared in the cloister and called to Felix.

"Oh, bodkins!" cried that youth in dismay, "I forgot all about my errand. My master will be in a dreadful passion when I get back. The yardstick will dance over my back just as lively as it used to when the world was flat. But I will stuff my jacket with dry grass." With these words he seized his bundle and hurried to where the Superior stood in the cloister.

"Reverend Father," he said, "here is your new cassock which Ignacio Diaz has sent to you."

"Very well," replied the priest. "Now, listen to me and carefully obey my directions. When you return to Palos, go at once to the house of the physician, Garcia Fernandez. Give him my compliments, and say that I request him to come to La Rabida at an early hour to-morrow, on business of the highest importance. Here is a letter for him which will explain it. Be careful and give it to no one but the doctor himself. Do you understand?"

"Yes, Father."

"Very well. Go now, for you should not vex your master by idle delay."

As Felix passed the porter's lodge, he saw Tortosa sitting with his crossbow in his hands. The old soldier called to him, —

"Does that dog seem quiet yet, Felix?"

"He has just chased the Superior's cat upon the wall," replied Felix, a little mischievously.

"Ah-h!" gasped Tortosa. Then he continued eagerly, "But if he should hurt the cat, Father Juan Perez would hang him without mercy."

"What are you doing with your crossbow?" asked Felix.

"My trusty weapon shall not leave my hand till that dangerous beast has gone," groaned the soldier.

"Oh, Tortosa," cried Felix, suddenly, "did you know that the world is round?"

For a few moments the soldier gazed at the boy with silent terror. Then he roared, as he stretched out his hand for an arrow,—

"Hast thou been playing with the dog? Art thou infected with madness? Begone!" And Felix, who knew the old archer's extreme fear of mad dogs, fled at once, without waiting for any further discussion of geographical problems.

When Felix reached Palos, he hastened to execute the priest's commission, and then returned to the shop. His gloomy expectations in regard to the yardstick were almost forgotten in the remembrance of the strange boy who had so coolly announced such astonishing things.

When he entered, he saw that the disdainful cavalier was still there. But his attention was immediately drawn to Ignacio Diaz, whose face wore a look of dreadful meaning, and whose fat hand was already reaching for the well-worn stick.

"So you have been idling again," cried the tailor. "And where is the old cassock? Where is it, stupid? Answer me!"

"I — I — forgot to ask for it," stammered Felix; "but —"

"No more; 'tis sufficient. Pardon me, Señor, that I am obliged to correct an idle, disobedient scamp in your presence."

"Oh, proceed with the punishment; do not hesitate on my account," replied the cavalier, with his unpleasant laugh.

The yardstick was already executing circles in the air, when Felix cried out desperately, —

"But hear me speak, master, and you, too, Señor Caballéro. *The world is round!*"

The tailor dropped his stick and stepped back, with a look of fright on his face.

"Little heretic!" he gasped.

But the effect produced on the strange cavalier by the boy's announcement was very singular. He sprang out of the rude chair with such violence that a long rent appeared in his cloak. Ignoring that accident, he caught Felix by both arms and shook him till his teeth rattled.

"Where did you learn that? Speak!" he cried sternly, and shook the frightened boy again.

"At the convent, — at La Rabida," cried Felix, while the tailor looked on in astonishment.

"Who told you? Answer!"

"A boy, a stranger. He and his father came there. The boy said his father knew everything."

"What was his name? Quick!"

"His name was Co — Col—"

"*Columbus!*" cried the cavalier.

"Yes, Señor."

"Zooks!" cried the tailor. "Your Co-Col — what-d'ye-call-him, must be out of his senses. Was he a sick man, blockhead?"

"No," replied Felix. Then his countenance fell as he continued, "But Father Juan Perez told me to tell the doctor, Garcia Fernandez, to come out to the convent."

"Exactly. I told you so," cried the tailor with complacency.

"When is he going out?" asked the stranger, tightening his grip again.

"To-morrow morning."

"Good."

The cavalier gave Felix a rude push. Then he said calmly, —

"Ah, I have torn my cloak. Here, boy, mend it for me, and I will give thee a ducat."

He flung the garment to Felix, who at once mounted his table and threaded his needle.

He took up the cloak, which was of costly cloth and scented with a peculiar and agreeable perfume.

When the rent was neatly mended, the cavalier threw the cloak over his shoulders and carelessly tossed to Felix two ducats.

"There is another for the fright I caused thee," he said, and left the shop without further words.

When he had gone, Ignacio Diaz pounced upon his apprentice and took possession of the ducats.

"He gave them to me," protested Felix.

"To thee, small animal! What need hast thou for ducats? Be thankful that I do not take down the yardstick again. Here, sew up these doublet seams. In the morning, when thou hast finished them, go to La Rabida and get the old cassock. Forget it again and I will flay thee. But, hark thee, while there learn what thou canst of this crazy stranger."

Felix could hardly close his eyes that night. He was thinking of his amiable new acquaintance, Diego Columbus, who had called him *caballéro*. He longed for the morning, when he could finish his seams and hasten to the convent.

CHAPTER II.

FELIX WINS THE CROSSBOW.

EARLY the next morning, Felix sprang from his bed and began his usual task of sweeping the shop. Hitherto he had been a great sluggard. Often had the angry tailor awakened him in a very sudden and painful manner. He had lived like a young animal, without ambition or thought for the future. But now a grand idea was germinating in his mind.

"What miracle has been wrought in thee?" cried Ignacio Diaz, when he entered the shop and saw the place clean and in order, and Felix already at work. But he continued, with a frown, "Don't think thou canst hide anything from me. I see thou art planning to ask for a holiday."

A little later in the morning the physician, Garcia Fernandez, emerged from his house, and was about to mount his mule and set out for the convent, when a cavalier in a cloak and green doublet approached and saluted him.

"Señor Fernandez," he said, "do not be surprised that I know your destination this morning. I learned it by a happy accident. You are about to visit one of the most learned men of this age, Señor Columbus, who has not yet received the distinction he merits. Though I am not personally acquainted with him, I have heard of his sublime projects, and I ask, as a great favor, that you permit me to accompany you to the convent of La Rabida, that I may meet the man for whom I have a great admiration. My name is Don Juan Vascoña."

"I do not know you," replied the physician bluntly; "but you seem to know more of this Columbus than I know. You may go with me to La Rabida if you wish. Señor Columbus will please himself about receiving you. Have you a mule?"

"I thank you, Señor. My horse is waiting in the next street."

In a few moments the cavalier returned,

mounted on a fine black horse, and he and the physician set out together for the convent.

Leaving their animals at the gate, they were admitted by Tortosa, who saluted Señor Fernandez with respectful familiarity.

"Where is Father Juan Perez?" asked the physician.

"I think he is with the strange man who came yesterday, Señor," replied Tortosa. "I suspect you are wanted, Doctor," he continued, tapping his head mysteriously. "The brothers have been telling me queer tales about him. They say the poor man thinks that the world is round like an orange!"

The physician burst into a loud laugh. Bending forward, he said to the porter in an impressive whisper, —

"And what if the world *is* round?"

"Santa Maria! You are fond of joking, Señor," muttered Tortosa, crossing himself. Suddenly he retreated into his lodge, as he saw Diego and his dog approaching.

"Pass on, Señores," he said. "There is the poor man's son. He will conduct you to his father. May the saints hasten his recovery."

The doctor laughed again, and crossed the courtyard to meet Diego, followed by Vascoña.

"Good morning, my boy," said the physician. "Will you conduct us to your father, Señor Columbus?"

"Yes, Señor," replied Diego, promptly wheeling about to lead the way. As Fernandez followed him through the cloister, he heard Vascoña call out, —

"Hold, Señor, bid the boy call off this beastly dog."

Looking back, they saw the bloodhound planted in Vascoña's path, bristling, and uttering low growls whenever the cavalier tried to advance.

"Perrito! What are you about? Come here!" called Diego, stamping his foot.

The dog, after casting several wistful glances from his master to Vascoña, turned and trotted back to Diego, wagging his tail

solemnly, as if to say, I have done my duty. I now leave the responsibility with you.

In a few moments Diego ushered the two gentlemen into a large apartment opening off the cloister. A heavy table stood in the centre of the room, and at this table were seated four men earnestly poring over a number of maps and charts. One was Father Juan Perez, pale and scholarly. Another, with powerful figure and bronzed features, was Martin Alonzo Pinzon, the wealthy and enterprising sea captain of Palos. The third, able, intelligent, and alert, was Sebastian Rodriguez, the celebrated pilot. The fourth was Christopher Columbus. With his noble white head and commanding form, he was the most striking figure of the group. His gray eyes were flashing with enthusiasm as he unfolded his plans to his auditors.

The physician's entrance was hailed with joy, for his scientific attainments had placed him high in the estimation of his friends. But they all gazed at Vascoña with surprise and questioning looks.

The cavalier, observing this, at once introduced himself, and addressed Columbus with fervid and artful eloquence, affirming the deep interest he had always taken in nautical science, and his intense desire to meet the learned Columbus, of whom he had heard so much. This, he said, must be his excuse for intruding upon them, but he trusted they would kindly permit him to join in a discussion which interested him so deeply.

"Señor," replied Columbus, with a gracious and benignant smile, "I rejoice to meet one who loves science, and who desires further knowledge. There is nothing here which we wish to conceal from honest men. Join our circle, if you wish, and freely discuss these great problems with us."

Fernandez and Vascoña took seats at the table, and Columbus proceeded to explain his sublime theories of our world, the greatness of which even he never fully comprehended.

In the midst of the discussion, Vascoña rose and approached Columbus in order better to see a chart which the latter was explaining. When he resumed his seat, he observed that Columbus had suddenly become silent and was regarding him with a grave and searching look. As the company noted this with surprise, Columbus spoke, —

"Señor Vascoña, I beg that you will not be offended, nor take it as a reflection on yourself; but I must request that you withdraw from this council."

"How, Señor!" cried Vascoña, springing up, "this is an insult."

"No, do not regard it so," returned Columbus calmly and gravely. "But I remain firm in my demand. If you refuse, then this discussion must end."

The cavalier was very angry, and furious words seemed about to burst from his lips; but, restraining himself with a great effort, he said, —

"This is singular usage, and I would be justified in demanding satisfaction; but I will comply with your capricious request."

Taking his broad hat, he stepped to the door.

"Señor," said Father Juan Perez, who felt sorry for the cavalier, "the convent is yours. Pray repose yourself in the garden, and join us at dinner."

"Thanks, I shall return to Palos," replied Vascoña haughtily, as he left the room.

"Señores," said Columbus, after a pause, "my treatment of the young gentleman may have seemed capricious. Nevertheless, I had a reason for it. I think you are all aware of the intense jealousy with which the king of Portugal regarded my application to the Court of Spain, and of his endeavors to have me return to him. He has spies at the Spanish Court who keep him well informed of what passes there. When this young cavalier approached me to look at the map, I detected a perfume about his dress which is much used by the dandies of the Portuguese Court. My suspicions were aroused, and I deemed it best to exclude a possible emissary of Portugal from our conference."

The others expressed their surprise and satisfaction, and the discussion was resumed.

Meanwhile Felix had finished his morning work with a rapidity that deeply astonished Ignacio Diaz, and the tailor began to indulge in pleasant calculations of his possible gains, provided his apprentice's fit of industry endured.

At last Felix, in high spirits, set out for the convent to get the Superior's old cassock. Tortosa admitted him. The soldier had his crossbow in hand.

"Ha, Felix!" he cried suspiciously, "dost thou feel perfectly well this morning?"

"I never felt better," replied Felix, laughing. "Where is Father Juan Perez? I want to get his old cassock."

"Alas! he is with the poor sick gentleman. Dr. Garcia Fernandez has just come to see him. Another gentleman came with the doctor; no doubt he is a notary summoned to write the poor man's will. Yet I don't see what he has to bequeath, except a good name, for every one can see that he is a true gentleman. Well, a good name is a blessed legacy. But thou wouldst best not disturb them now."

"What! is Señor Columbus sick?" cried Felix.

"Here, here," said Tortosa, tapping his forehead. "He believes that the world is round."

"Perhaps the world *is* round," replied Felix boldly.

"No more of that," cried Tortosa severely. "I love a harmless joke, but that is rank blasphemy."

"Where is his son, Diego?" asked Felix, avoiding the dangerous subject.

"Oh, he is about with that terrible dog. Thou shouldst have heard the brute snarl at the fine young gentleman who came with the doctor Fernandez. I took down my crossbow in a hurry."

"Come, Tortosa," cried Felix, "let us go and find the boy. I like him well, and he must be lonely here. Let us shoot at a mark with your crossbow."

After some demur, Tortosa consented, and they went to the garden, where they found Diego seated on a bench, with his dog at his feet. On the top of the garden wall sat the big black cat intently watching the intruders on his domain.

"Good morning, Señor," called Felix, joyously.

"How do you do, *caballéro*," responded Diego, in his gentle, pleasant tones.

"Can you send your dog away?" asked Felix. "Tortosa doesn't like dogs; and if you will, he'll let us shoot at a mark with his crossbow."

"Very well," said Diego; and taking the dog over into the cloister, he placed his cap on the floor, and bade him watch it, and then returned to Tortosa and Felix.

Felix now placed a mark against a bank of earth near the fountain, and the three took turns in shooting. The bow was powerful, the string being drawn back by a winch, and it shot an arrow with prodigious force.

Tortosa, who had carried the weapon through many campaigns, was an expert

FELIX WINS THE CROSSBOW.

marksman; and Felix, who had sometimes practised with him, could make some creditable shots. But the sport was new to Diego, and his arrows flew about at random.

While they were thus pleasantly engaged, a sound of distant shouts and screams was borne to their ears. After listening a moment, Tortosa said that he would go and see what it meant. He returned to the gate, and the boys followed him.

As they stepped outside, a frightful scene met their eyes. A mad dog came rushing across the open ground in front of the convent, followed at a distance by a yelling rabble armed with clubs and pitchforks.

The animal was howling and frothing at the mouth in a dreadful manner, and he came along with great speed directly toward Tortosa and the boys as they stood at the gate.

Tortosa, who had coolly stood in the front of a score of battles when the air was dark with whizzing missiles, and who had climbed many a bloody scaling-ladder as if going to a feast, was horror-struck by this one danger that he dreaded, and stood like a stone image.

"Back! Back inside, and shut the gate," screamed Felix, seizing Tortosa's arm. But at that moment a fresh alarm was added. Perrito, who could not bear to be left behind, had slowly followed them, bringing Diego's cap in his mouth. Hearing the uproar, he darted out of the gate and stood glaring at the mad animal approaching him, and quivering in the act of rushing forward to meet him.

Diego, realizing the danger, threw himself forward and clasped Perrito around the neck. It happened that Felix had the crossbow in his hand, he having been about to shoot when they heard the outcry. Now he saw that this was their only salvation. Quickly he placed an arrow on the string, and clapped the stock against his breast. His muscles seemed to harden like steel. There was a sharp twang. The arrow pierced the mad dog's breast, and the poor beast rolled lifeless on the ground.

Pale with fright, Diego dragged Perrito inside the gate. The people approached and gazed at the dead dog, and finally dragged him away to bury him.

Felix, trembling a little now the danger was over, handed the crossbow to Tortosa. The soldier's brown face flushed as he answered bluntly, and with a sort of emotion, —

"Keep it."

"It is your turn to shoot," said Felix.

The soldier seemed surprised at his coolness. He laid his hand on the boy's shoulder and said gravely, —

"Thou hast done a brave deed. My crossbow is thine. Thou hast won it."

Tortosa was evidently humiliated at having lost his presence of mind at the moment of danger. Felix blushed with pleasure. To be praised was a new experience to him. He could hardly realize that the veteran archer had actually given him the crossbow that he had borne in the wars of Spain.

Presently they all returned to the garden and sat on a bench by the fountain, and Tortosa, in a subdued voice, began to tell the boys old legends of the convent concerning mad dogs, and the miraculous way in which the evil was allayed in ancient times.

"A long time ago," he said, "there was a terrible plague of mad dogs in this part of Andalusia. It is very bad now, but it was a great deal worse then. At last a very good and pious monk placed an image of the Madonna in the chapel of the convent, and it was called 'Our Lady of Rabida.'

"So great was the power of this image that the evil of mad dogs was almost entirely put an end to, and great was the joy of the people.

"Then came the dreadful time when the Moors invaded Spain and approached La Rabida. All the monks fled save one, who lingered, determined to save the sacred image. He bore it from the chapel and buried it in the ground. But before he could escape, the Moors came and captured him. They thought he had been burying treasure, and tried to make him reveal the hiding-place; and as he would not do it, they cut off his head with a scimiter.

"The image has never been found, and the brothers of the convent say that the ghost of the monk still walks the cloisters at night, and will always do so until Our

Lady of Rabida is found and restored to the chapel."

"Have you ever seen the ghost?" asked Felix breathlessly.

"Do you believe it?" inquired Diego calmly.

"I have never seen it," replied Tortosa, "but I don't like to walk in the cloisters late at night. I wish that the image might be found so that the monk could rest in peace, and there would be an end to madness in dogs."

At that moment Perrito, whom Diego had left in the cloister, came slowly toward them, snuffing the air and giving an occasional low growl.

"See that dog!" cried Tortosa, rising to his feet in alarm. "He's coming this way. Call him off, Diego."

"No," replied Diego, "he will not touch you. I don't understand what he means. Let us watch him."

"Mad, most likely," muttered Tortosa apprehensively.

The dog continued to advance till he had passed the bench and stood beside a thick clump of shubbery a few feet away. Suddenly, with a loud bay, he charged into the bushes, and instantly a violent combat took place there. The fierce growls of the dog were mingled with the loud imprecations of a man.

Tortosa and the boys sprang forward,

and at the same moment Señor Vascoña and Perrito tumbled out of the bushes, the cavalier kicking and struggling and reaching for his sword, while the dog held him firmly by the arm.

Diego ran forward and with difficulty made Perrito loosen his hold, and dragged him away. The cavalier drew his sword and furiously advanced to run the dog through. Tortosa at once confronted him, with the coolness of an old soldier, and said, —

"Put up your sword, Señor. Why were you concealed in the garden?"

At that moment Columbus and his companions appeared, having heard the outcry and the struggle. They were soon apprised of the cause of the tumult. Vascoña cried angrily, —

"I had the reverend Father's permission to walk in this garden, and overhearing the porter telling an idle tale to the boys, I paused to listen, and then that savage dog attacked me."

"I regret, Señor," replied Father Juan Perez, with cool courtesy, "that you have not had a pleasanter visit to La Rabida. But as it is, the best we can do is to bid you God-speed. Adieu, Señor; I trust the occasion of our next meeting may be more agreeable."

Thus being dismissed, the cavalier swallowed his anger as well as he could and haughtily departed; and presently they heard the clatter of his horse's hoofs on the road.

This matter being concluded, Columbus and his friends resumed their conversation. Father Juan Perez handed a letter to the pilot, Sebastian Rodriguez, and said, —

"Señor Rodriguez, you will deliver my letter to the queen again beseeching her Highness to favor the project of Señor Columbus. No one could perform the mission better."

"I shall depart this very night," replied Rodriguez.

Felix had bade Diego good-by, and was accompanying Tortosa to the gate. He again offered the archer his crossbow, but Tortosa assured him that it was his. Felix then requested him to keep it for him, lest the tailor should seize and sell it.

Felix had nearly reached Palos before it occurred to him that he had again forgotten to ask for the old cassock.

He knew that Ignacio Diaz was very curious. With the cunning that tyranny had taught him, he resolved to burst into the shop and overwhelm his master with a startling and lurid tale of the day's adventures, and so avoid his ancient enemy that hung on the wall.

CHAPTER III.

A ROYAL MESSENGER.

Two weeks passed without any tidings from the messenger to the Court. Ignacio Diaz had not sent Felix again to La Rabida. The old cassock, he thought, would furnish an excuse to send him when the pilot had returned and the news might be obtained.

But one day Diaz, standing in the door of his shop, saw Sebastian Rodriguez ride by on a mule and take the road to the convent.

"Felix," cried the tailor, "Señor Rodriguez has returned. He is going to La Rabida. Follow him at once, and find out, if thou canst, the result of this application to the queen. And — Oh, yes, get the old cassock, do you hear?"

Felix, very well pleased that the tailor's curiosity was giving him a half-holiday, was soon on his way to the convent.

When he arrived, Tortosa informed him that Fernandez, Pinzon, Rodriguez, Father Juan Perez, and Columbus were all in earnest and excited council together, and that the message brought by the pilot seemed to have pleased them all very much.

Felix and Tortosa went to the garden, where they found Diego and Perrito. The Superior's big cat sat on the top of the wall as usual sunning himself and keeping one eye on the dog, and the other on a noisy flock of blackbirds in a fig-tree near by.

Tortosa sat down on a bench, with Felix on one side and Diego on the other, and told them tales of battles and sieges.

Then Felix ran to fetch the crossbow, and they began shooting at a mark. Their hearts were light, and the sport went merrily on, until it was suddenly cut short by a dismal catastrophe.

Diego could not handle the crossbow very well, and his arrows usually flew wide of the mark. At last one of these unlucky shafts, flying across the garden, glanced on the bole of a lemon-tree and darted off at a sharp angle. The unfortunate cat happened to be lying in its path and was instantly transfixed. He gave a wild leap and fell to the ground, dead.

There was the deepest consternation among the archers. Even the veteran Tortosa turned pale. They went over and stood around the body of the unlucky cat.

"This is very bad," muttered Tortosa at last. "The Superior will be terribly angry. This cat formerly belonged to his aged uncle, whom he regarded with the greatest veneration. The old gentleman went to glory three years ago, and left the Superior his money and his cat, charging him to care for the beast as if it were his own child. And he has done so. The brothers here once told me of a poor monk who struck the cat one day with a willow switch because he jumped on the table in the refectory and lapped all the cream off the milk. As a penance for striking the cat, Father Juan Perez made the monk go on a pilgrimage with peas in his shoes, and they say he hasn't got back yet. So, ever since, the brothers have had the milk, and the cat has had the cream."

"Oh, what will he do to me! What shall I do?" cried Diego, in distress.

"Very likely he will not help your father any more, and turn you both out of the convent. It might be worse than that, too," said Felix gloomily.

"Oh, this is dreadful!" sighed Diego. "My poor father,—and the poor cat. Why did I ever shoot the arrow!"

"Listen," whispered Tortosa, tragically. "Let us bury the cat in the garden, and no one will be the wiser."

They looked at one another with agitation.

"Would it be right?" murmured Diego.

If not an honest way out of the difficulty, it certainly seemed the easiest. But this little plan suddenly became impracticable. A heavy step was heard behind them, and turning in alarm they beheld Father Torribio, one of the prefects of the convent, a cold, stern, implacable man. A dark frown was on his face, and he surveyed the trembling group with fierce eyes.

"Who has done this?" he asked harshly. "Who has shot the Superior's cat? Answer me, Lorenzo Tortosa, instantly!"

"I was just — just reproving the boys," stammered Tortosa.

"Who shot the cat?" repeated the prefect angrily.

"I did," said Felix, courageously stepping forward.

"Thou bold rascal!" cried the prefect, seizing him by the arm. "Come with me. Thou shalt receive an hundred lashes, and be sent to the gaol."

With these ominous words, he dragged Felix away and locked him up in a dark cell, where he remained for what seemed a long time in fear and suspense.

When night had fallen, the door of Felix's prison was suddenly opened and one of the brothers or inferiors of the convent entered hastily, holding in one hand a taper which he carefully shaded with the other. Felix gazed at him with fear, thinking that he might have been sent to bring him to punishment; but the brother, after regarding him for a moment, gave a short laugh and said, —

"Little brother, thou hast done us a great service. Thou hast slain our tyrant. Now, thank heaven we shall sit at the second table. Hitherto it has been, first, the Fathers, then the cat, and lastly, we poor sinners. Come with me and I will see thee safely out of the gate, for I and my companions would not see thee abandoned to the anger of Father Torribio."

With these words the monk led the way into the cloisters and thence to the gate, where Tortosa was waiting to let Felix out.

"Make thy little legs fly, brother," whispered the jovial monk, as he departed.

Felix did not return to Palos, but turned his face in the direction of Granada, at that time the scene of fierce war between the Spaniards and the Moors. Although he had boldly taken upon himself the blame for the

death of the cat, yet he felt terrified at the thought of the punishment that might fall upon him. He resolved to take final leave of all his old associations and seek his fortune elsewhere. He regretted that he had not asked Tortosa for the crossbow.

He walked for the greater part of the night, lighted on his way by a brilliant moon. Towards morning, hungry and weary, he lay down under a tree by the roadside and fell asleep.

When he awoke, the moon, now growing pale, hung over the mountains in the west, and the pure morning light was streaming over the earth. A man holding a mule by the bridle stood beside him. Felix sat up and gazed at the stranger with surprise. The next moment he recoiled with a sensation of fear. The man was Father Juan Perez.

"Where art thou going, Felix?" asked the priest, in a gentle voice.

"I — I don't know," stammered Felix.

"Thou art fleeing from punishment," said Juan Perez. "Didst thou kill my cat?"

"Yes," murmured Felix.

"Son," said the priest, laying his hand kindly on the boy's head, "I admire thy generous courage in trying to save thy companion at thy own expense, but I must blame thee for thy falsehood. I saw the whole affair from the cloisters, and know that it was the son of Columbus who killed the cat.

"When I heard thee avow the act, I remained silent, desiring to see how the boy would bear himself in the matter. Had he said nothing, and let the punishment fall on an innocent person, my zeal for Columbus would have waned, for I should have suspected the father of such a son. But before night, Diego came to me and confessed everything, and begged that thou shouldst be set at liberty.

"I was then preparing to set out for Court in obedience to the command of her Highness Queen Isabella. Forgetting thee, I left the convent at midnight, and have travelled all night, much regretting that I had not informed Father Torribio of thy innocence. But only a few moments ago I was surprised to find thee sleeping under this tree."

Felix sprang up with a heavy load removed from his spirits. But a sudden fear for Diego and his father checked his joy.

"I hope you will not punish Diego," he said. "He did not mean to do it."

"The consequences of the accident are somewhat serious to me," said Juan Perez.

"According to the singular terms of my uncle's will, the convent loses a large sum of money by the violent death of the cat. Nevertheless, I have pardoned the boy. He is brave and conscientious."

The priest reflected a moment, and then asked, —

"How didst thou escape?"

Felix hung his head and replied, —

"I would rather not tell."

"Very well, child," said the kind priest, "I will not press thee. Perhaps it is better that thou shouldst not return immediately, as Father Torribio, not being aware of thy innocence, might treat thee harshly. Come with me. After reaching Court, I may need a trusty messenger to return to Palos."

The priest mounted his mule, and Felix walked beside him, and they soon reached a village where they breakfasted with the parish priest, who received them very hospitably.

Here Juan Perez obtained a donkey for Felix to ride, and presently they resumed their journey. Felix was very much elated at the turn his affairs had taken.

After travelling three days, they entered the Vega of Granada, and riding over a wide plain, devastated by war, reached the military city of Santa Fé, built by Ferdinand and Isabella while besieging the city of Granada.

Looming dimly in the smoky atmosphere,  they saw the far extending walls of the besieged city. At a distance they heard the heavy detonations of cannon. Troops, and intrenchments, and engines of war appeared on every side. In a low, dark building Felix saw a multitude of wounded men, and dismal groans of pain came to his ears. Several dead soldiers lay beside the road, their white faces turned upward.

Through these dreadful sights and sounds they rode, and reached a chapel and convent where dwelt a company of Franciscan monks. Hastening from the awful atmosphere of war, they entered a cool, dusky, quiet courtyard, where the friars welcomed them kindly, and led them away to repose after the fatigues of their journey.

Here Felix quietly resided for several days among the monks, while Father Juan Perez entered the presence of the sovereigns to plead the cause of Columbus.

The monks were very kind to Felix. He ate with them in the refectory, and they tried to amuse him as well as they could. One of them took him about the warlike city, and he saw the king and queen ride by in armor, attended by a brilliant cavalcade of knights and officers.

One evening Father Juan Perez returned to the convent and called Felix to his side.

"My child," he said, "the time has come when thou canst do me a service. I must remain here for a time. Canst thou faithfully bear a message to Palos?"

"I will try," replied Felix, promptly.

"Very well. I will trust thee," said the priest. "Be ready to start early to-morrow morning. Thou mayst ride my mule."

At an early hour the next morning Felix sat on his mule in the courtyard receiving the final directions of Father Juan Perez.

"Here is a letter for Señor Columbus," said the priest. "Deliver it to the physician, Garcia Fernandez, who will take it to him.

"Now, attend carefully. Here is a package of money, — twenty thousand maravedis in florins, — which her Highness Queen Isabella sends to Señor Columbus. Child, this is a proud day for thee. Thou art a royal messenger. Consider how faithful thou shouldst be to deserve this great honor. Here is money for thy expenses on the road, and this note for Father Torribio certifying to thy innocence in regard to the cat. Now, go, and God be with thee."

Bidding adieu to the kind monks, Felix set forth on his journey, with a feeling of vast importance at the thought that he was a royal messenger. To what honor he had arisen in a few days! He began to regard the dingy shop of Ignacio Diaz as a butterfly might regard its chrysalis. But in the midst of his glory it occurred to Felix that a few more days might see him again seated on his table, in disagreeable proximity to the dancing yardstick.

He met with no accident on his journey, though he guarded his letters and money with an excessive care that would certainly have awakened the suspicions of shrewd thieves, had he met any. In due time he triumphantly rode into Palos, and dismounted at the door of the physician, Garcia Fernandez.

The doctor was ill and sore, having unfortunately fallen from his mule the day before, but he hobbled to the door with some excitement to receive the packets from Father Juan Perez.

As Felix stood at the door while Garcia Fernandez read his letter, he heard a stealthy step, and his arms were suddenly seized from behind. Somewhat startled he struggled with his captor, and, twisting about, saw his master, Ignacio Diaz.

"Ah, thou villain, — thou runaway! Where hast thou been these ten days? Is this the way thou bringest me the news — the old cassock, I mean? Come with me, jackanapes. The yardstick will loosen thy tongue. Come, I say!"

At that moment the tailor was petrified by a terrible voice, — the voice of Garcia Fernandez.

"Do you court the rack or the gallows, tailor? You have assaulted a royal messenger. Release him, instantly."

"Wh-what!" stammered the tailor, with amazement.

"Felix is at present a royal messenger. You would better not interfere with him."

The tailor stumbled backward, took off his hat and bowed several times, saying to Felix obsequiously, —

"I did not know it. I meant no harm, sir. Believe me, I meant no harm." Then he remained staring at his apprentice, while the physician calmly resumed his reading.

When Garcia Fernandez had finished the letters, he said to Felix, —

"My boy, you must take the letter and money to Señor Columbus at La Rabida. I am so lame that I cannot go out to-day. Hasten, for you bear good news."

As Felix again mounted his mule, he noticed a man wrapped in a cloak leaning against the wall near by. His hat covered his face, but for an instant, from beneath the broad-laced brim, Felix caught the keen black eyes of Don Juan Vascoña fixed upon him. Then he rode away toward the convent.

As he dismounted at the gate of La Rabida, Tortosa emerged from his lodge and gazed at him with astonishment. He hurried out and embraced Felix joyfully.

"Where dost thou come from, Felix? Oh, but I shiver to see thee here! Father Torribio is in a fearful rage. Thou wouldst best skip it away again. Is it the Superior's mule. Where is Father Juan Perez?"

"He is at Court, and I went with him,"

replied Felix, full of excitement. "He sent me back with a letter for Señor Columbus. Where is he?"

"Marvellous!" cried Tortosa. "Ah, the poor man will be glad to see thee. Let us go find him."

They hastened to the garden, where they found Columbus and Diego. Felix hurried forward with vast importance and saluted Columbus.

"Señor," he said, "I come from Father Juan Perez, who is now at Court. He has sent this letter to you. Her Highness Queen Isabella sends you this package of money."

Columbus took the packets with deep emotion. His hands trembled, and he was very pale. But his mind was diverted for a moment from these matters of supreme importance, as Felix continued, with a worldly shrewdness that he had learned from the customers of Ignacio Diaz,—

"Please give me a receipt for them, Señor."

Columbus smiled, and overcame his agitation. He swiftly wrote a receipt and handed it to Felix, who gazed at it with awe, for he could not read it. Columbus hurriedly opened his letters.

"Felix," whispered Tortosa and Diego, almost at the same moment, "come, we have something most wonderful to tell thee."

Felix stepped aside with them, and Tortosa hastened to tell his story.

"The next day after thy departure," he said, "I took my spade and went to bury the Superior's cat. I dug a grave under an orange-tree, and while I was digging, the spade struck something hard. I cleared away the loose earth and looked down.

"Then the few poor hairs that are left on my pate stood straight up, for there was a white face looking up at me from the bottom of the hole. I went away, but as I stopped to cross myself, a sudden thought turned me back and set me to digging like a giant. In a few moments I had uncovered the image of Our Lady of Rabida, — buried ever since the invasion of the Moors, — a little soiled and disfigured, but sound and whole, thank heaven.

"Soon the whole convent was on the spot, and she was borne in triumph to the chapel. Ha, ha! No more madness in dogs. I need not fear Perrito now."

While Felix was expressing his wonder and congratulations at this strange recovery, they heard the voice of Columbus. He was gazing upward and murmuring thanks to God. Diego ran to his side. Columbus embraced him, and cried joyfully, —

"Joy, my dear Diego. The queen has sent for me." They went away together.

At that moment an iron grip closed on Felix's arm, and the harsh voice of Father Torribio said, —

"What! thou impudent wretch! Darest thou return and defy me?"

Felix at once presented the note from Father Juan Perez. Father Torribio read it, frowning. Then he said, —

"Very well, if thou art innocent. But thou must answer one question. Who released thee from the cell?"

"I would rather not tell."

"Thou *must* tell. It is my duty to find out, and I never neglect my duty. Tell me,

A ROYAL MESSENGER.

or I shall imprison thee on bread and water till thou dost."

"I cannot tell," replied Felix firmly.

So presently the royal messenger was marched away and ignominiously locked up in a cell adjoining Father Torribio's, where no kindly disposed brother could rescue him; and there he supped all alone on dry bread and pure, cold water.

CHAPTER IV.

THE MONK'S GHOST.

WHEN Columbus learned that Felix was imprisoned, he earnestly interceded for him, but in vain. The stern priest was inflexible.

But the next day Columbus met Father Torribio in the cloisters and informed him of his intention to depart for the Court as soon as he could conclude the necessary preparations.

"I am going to Palos to purchase clothing and a mule," he said. "I would ask that the boy Felix be permitted to accompany me, as I wish him to direct me to suitable markets in the town."

"He is undergoing discipline," replied Father Torribio grimly. "I can send with you one of the brothers who can furnish you the necessary information."

"I must have Felix," insisted Columbus, "as I wish also to converse with him in regard to his visit to Granada."

"Very well, Señor," replied Father Torribio, who hesitated to oppose a man who had been summoned to the presence of Queen Isabella. "But I must hold you responsible for his return."

So in a few moments Felix was delivered to Columbus, who greeted him with a kindly smile, and presently they set out on foot for Palos.

"Felix," whispered Tortosa, as they passed the lodge, "Señor Columbus is a good, kind-hearted gentleman. What a pity it is that he has got that queer whim in his head about the world being round!"

On the way to Palos, Columbus talked very kindly to Felix, who thought Diego very fortunate in possessing such a father. When they entered the town, Columbus paused at the door of an inn, and giving Felix a florin, said, —

"This is in payment for thy services to-day. I will leave thee here for a time. Enter the inn and refresh thyself as thou wilt. I fear thou hast suffered a fast day not in the calendar."

"I do not wish the money," replied Felix. "I am glad to serve you, Señor."

"Take it," said Columbus. "Thou shalt not serve me for nothing." And putting the coin in the boy's hand, he went away.

About an hour later Columbus returned mounted on a fine mule that he had just purchased. He found Felix sitting in the sun, and a certain rotundity and ruddiness in the boy's appearance assured him that the pantry of the inn furnished something better than bread and water.

"Felix," said Columbus, gravely but with a gleam of amusement in his eyes, "I notice a wondrous change in thee. Come, now, and show me a tailor's shop, for I must buy a suit of clothing."

"A tailor's shop!" cried Felix. "I can lead you to the shop of my master, Ignacio Diaz."

"Ah, I remember. Diego told me that thou art a tailor's boy. Very well. Is thy master honest? Has he good cloth?"

"He has good cloth, but he will charge you too much for it. And when people pay him, they always ask for a receipt."

"Thy recommendation is rather dubious, I think. But lead on. We will see the goods of Señor Diaz."

They soon reached the shop, and were received very obsequiously by the tailor. Felix had evidently risen considerably in his master's estimation, and he expressed his sense of the importance of his customer by asking three times the proper price for the suit selected by Columbus.

And when Columbus paid the amount asked without question, and without demanding a receipt, Felix himself was surprised, and Ignacio Diaz was fully assured of the correctness of his own judgment.

"Felix," whispered the tailor, drawing his apprentice aside, "thou hast fallen in with rich and influential friends. Doubtless thou hast secured a fine position. I trust thou wilt remember that something is due me if I release thee. One hundred ducats will be a reasonable sum. Wilt thou speak to thy employers about it?"

After a little hesitation, Felix informed his master that his fortunes were really the reverse of brilliant, and that when he escaped from imprisonment on bread and water, he would be ready to return to work.

The tailor seemed much disappointed on hearing this, for the one hundred ducats had evidently figured very pleasingly in his thoughts of late.

After making a few more purchases, Columbus and Felix returned to the convent, and Felix was soon immured in his cell in company with a jug of water and a dry loaf.

But when he was alone, the beauties of forethought were exemplified. From his ample sash he extracted a quantity of cheese and cold pork, which he proceeded to feast upon with an appetite unimpaired by his remarkable performance at the dinner table of the inn.

The next day Columbus departed for the Court, and soon after a real time of trouble began for Felix.

Unfortunately the vigilant Father Torribio detected and confiscated the remnants of his smuggled provisions. This discovery excited the anger of the priest, and as Felix still refused to tell who had released him, he was subjected to actual starvation, receiving barely enough food to keep him alive. Yet he would not yield.

Father Torribio was not naturally cruel. He was intensely devoted, strictly honest and incorruptible, but bigoted, stern, undeviating in what he deemed to be his duty, and relentless to whomsoever opposed his authority. So poor Felix was in a dangerous position.

Two weeks passed. Tortosa and Diego laid a plot to smuggle food to Felix, but the vigilance of Father Torribio was too keen. Every day the priest made the brothers pass before the starving boy in order that he might point out the culprit.

Felix could hardly help smiling as he saw the apprehensive face of the jolly brother who had released him; but he maintained a stubborn silence, in spite of the dismal void within him.

One day Felix was lying half unconscious on his hard cot when he heard loud voices in Father Torribio's room. He sprang up and listened intently. To his great joy he recognized the clear, ringing tones of Father Juan Perez mingled with the deep voice of Father Torribio.

In a few moments the door of the cell was thrown open, and Juan Perez entered, followed by Diego and Tortosa.

"My child," cried Juan Perez, with tears in his eyes, "I did not dream that thou wouldst be so harshly dealt with. Tortosa, take him to thy lodge and give him food."

His exultant friends bore Felix away in triumph to the porter's lodge, and Tortosa gave him a cup of savory broth and a biscuit.

"More, more," cried Felix petulantly. "Are you, too, going to starve me? I'm going back to Palos."

He rose weakly as if to go, but Tortosa gently forced him back to his seat.

"Listen, Felix," he said. "I was once in a besieged city when the food gave out. Many died of hunger, but we never thought of surrender. At last an army came to our rescue. When food was given us I saw many men who had bravely endured hunger die from eating too much. So you must be patient, and you shall have plenty in good time. Here is a little more broth."

So Tortosa carefully fed his patient until he was fully restored. Then Felix returned to Ignacio Diaz, glad to leave the place where he had suffered hunger, which was more terrible than a wilderness of yardsticks. He resumed his place on the tailor's table, and for a brief period his existence fell back into the old grooves.

A few days after Felix returned to Palos, a singular experience befell Diego. The room which he and his father occupied as a sleeping apartment opened off a long corridor. It was large and bare, furnished only with two cots, a heavy wooden table, one or two chairs and a massive cabinet or secretary where Columbus kept his maps and charts, which were of great value. Many of them were the only copies extant, and their worth in money may be estimated by the fact that one hundred and thirty ducats were once paid for a single map made in

1439, — a sum equal to more than five hundred dollars at the present time.

One evening Diego walked with Perrito in the garden until the hour for locking up arrived. He retired to his bedchamber, leaving the dog as usual in the cloisters which opened on the garden.

He had felt very lonely since his father's departure. Juan Perez had informed him of Columbus's arrival at Court. But his stay there seemed likely to be indefinitely prolonged, for the siege of Granada was being vigorously conducted, and the attention of the king and queen was closely occupied with the pressing business of war.

Diego repeated his prayers, and lay down to sleep. Slumber came to him quickly, and "steeped his senses in forgetfulness."

He awoke in the dead of night. The moon had risen, and her pale light was pouring through the high, iron-barred window, filling the room with a mysterious radiance. The sound that had awakened him now came to his ears with increased volume. It was the loud, angry baying of Perrito.

All at once a shock of terror benumbed his body, while his mind awoke to intense alertness. A frightful figure stood in the middle of the room gazing at him, — the form of a monk with shaven head, pallid features, and large spectral eyes. A dark ring extended around his bare neck.

Tortosa's tale of the monk, who had been killed by the Moors, and whose ghost walked the cloisters, came to his mind. He believed that the awful visitant stood before him, and he was too terrified even to utter a prayer for protection.

Perrito's barking increased in fury. The figure moved slowly toward the door, keeping its staring eyes fixed on Diego.

At that moment he heard a shuffling step in the corridor, and the dim light of a taper was projected past the open door. In a moment Tortosa appeared, with a candle in one hand and the crossbow in the other.

"Diego," he cried, "is thy dog mad in spite of Our Lady of Rabida? Get up, I pray thee, and—*Santa Maria! Ow-w-w! Help! help!*"

His eyes had fallen upon the dreadful figure moving toward him. The candle fell from his hand and went out, the crossbow struck the floor with a startling clatter, and poor Tortosa followed it, and, flat on his face, called lustily on numerous saints for aid, while the spectre swept over him and vanished.

In a little while almost the entire convent, aroused by the shouts of Tortosa and the clamor of the dog, was gathered in the corridor, listening with wonder and horror to the incoherent recital of the porter, corroborated in its main points by Diego.

Nearly all the monks fully believed in the ghost, and they cast apprehensive glances over their shoulders, and carefully shielded their tapers or lamps, lest the draught should extinguish them.

Whatever Father Juan Perez really believed, he did not chide their credulous fear. He merely said, —

"Perchance the good monk wished to assure himself that Our Lady of Rabida had really been restored to her place. He will trouble us no more. Let us repair to the chapel and celebrate a mass for the repose of his soul."

The monks were well pleased not to retire to their lonely cells, and presently the chapel was lighted. The tall candles at the altar threw a soft light on the white image of Our Lady of Rabida, and the clear voice of Father Juan Perez was heard conducting the service.

The next morning as Felix was seated on his table busily sewing, the physician, Garcia Fernandez, hobbled into the shop, being still lame from his fall. Ignacio Diaz bowed servilely, scenting a possible order; but he was soon undeceived.

"Felix," said the physician, seating himself, "a messenger has brought me a letter from Señor Columbus to his son, and I wish you to take it at once to La Rabida."

At this the tailor drew a very long face, for since his return Felix had developed remarkable ambition and industry, and his absence meant a reduction of profits. Ignacio Diaz sincerely wished that Felix's new friends would either let him alone, or take him away altogether and pay him, Ignacio Diaz, one hundred ducats.

"Tailor," said the physician, throwing a ducat on the table, "here is medicine to remove that dismal expression from your face. I will pay you for the boy's time until he returns."

This was, perhaps, a rash bargain on the part of Garcia Fernandez, but it did not occur to him at the time.

Felix was soon ready to start for the convent, for he was glad at the prospect of seeing Diego again. He set out joyfully. The beautiful landscape shone in the morning sun. The blue ocean glittered. Again he saw the *Pinta* gliding up the Tinto like a white sea-bird.

When he arrived at the convent, Tortosa detained him at the gate to tell him the strange occurrence of the preceding night; and by that time the old soldier had succeeded in adding some striking embellishments to the original narrative.

Then they went to the garden, where they found Diego curiously watching the dog, who was walking about snuffing the air and uttering low growls.

"It is lucky that Our Lady of Rabida has been found," muttered Tortosa, looking suspiciously at the dog.

"Good morning, *caballéro*," cried Diego pleasantly, as he saw Felix approaching. "Perrito is trying to tell me something, but I am not bright enough to understand him. Oh, did Tortosa tell you about the ghost?"

"I have brought you a letter from your father," said Felix.

Diego hurried forward, took the package and opened it. As he read, his face assumed a serious and anxious expression. When he had finished the sheet, he glanced about him several times, and, seeing no one near, said, —

"My friends, I will read what my father has written to me. His good fortune seems ever delayed.

"'My dear Son : — I came hither safely, and soon after my arrival obtained an audience of her Highness Queen Isabella. But the sovereigns are too much engrossed with the siege now progressing to give attention to my business at present. After the surrender of the city, which seems probable, I trust my affairs may progress more favorably.

"'I am living with my good friend, Alonzo de Quintanilla, who always aids me to the extent of his ability.

"'I write you at this time more especially to give you warning touching a certain matter. You are fully aware of the constant jealousy of the king of Portugal since my application to the Court of Spain. I am informed that a Portuguese emissary has been sent to Palos to be a spy upon me and to retard my business as much as possible.

"'Be vigilant and circumspect regarding any suspicious person. More particularly, guard with great care the maps and charts I left with you. Their loss would be irreparable.

"'I suppose you are again pursuing your studies under the kind direction of Father Juan Perez. Be faithful and persevere.

"'I trust our young friend, Felix Madrigal, is now at liberty. We are deeply indebted to him, and if I am successful he shall not be forgotten.'"

Diego looked at Felix, smiling.

"In debt to me?" cried Felix with surprise.

"Did you not save Perrito and me from the mad dog? Did you not take the blame of the cat's death? Did you not carry the queen's message?" asked Diego gently.

Felix blushed and was silent. Suddenly he asked, earnestly, —

"Are the charts safe?"

"Yes," replied Diego. "They are all in the secretary in our bedchamber."

"Have you looked at them this morning?"

"No, but I looked at them yesterday."

Perrito had been roaming the garden, and now he gave a long bay, with his nose in the air.

"What ails the dog?" cried Diego. "He has acted in that way all this morning."

Tortosa began to sidle away.

"Did you see the ghost in your room?" asked Felix gravely.

THE MONK'S GHOST.

"Yes. Both Tortosa and I saw it. 'Twas a dreadful spectacle."

"Diego," cried Felix, with agitation, "let us go and look at the charts."

"Why, do you think the monk's ghost would steal my father's charts?" asked Diego, surprised.

Felix did not reply, and they passed through the corridors to Diego's room. Diego opened the secretary, and uttered an exclamation of fright. The charts were gone!

"Where are they? Who has taken them?" he cried, wildly wringing his hands.

Felix thrust his head into the secretary and remained motionless for a moment. Then he stepped back with a peculiar look.

"Do you smell anything?" he asked.

"No," replied Diego, pausing in his lamentations. "What is it?"

"That Portuguese spy has been here," cried Felix. "I mended his cloak once, and I know that queer scent. I smelt it the moment you opened the door. It was the same man that Perrito caught hidden in the garden. I believe he heard Tortosa's story about the monk and the Moors, and has played the ghost so that he could steal the charts. What the mischief was his name?"

"Don Juan Vascoña!" cried Diego, very pale. "What shall I do? What will my father say? The charts are lost!"

"No, they are *not* lost!" cried Felix boldly. "We must catch that fellow. He will not burn the charts; he will take them to the king of Portugal."

"Yes, catch him!" roared Tortosa, starting forward fiercely.

"But how?" groaned Diego.

How, indeed! Vascoña had a long start, and, on his fleet horse, was probably far on his way to Lisbon.

CHAPTER V.

THE PURSUIT.

"I must inform Father Juan Perez at once," cried Diego; and he darted from the room.

"Alas!" muttered Tortosa, "I will barter my head for a watermelon. There the villain stood before me, and I with the crossbow in hand, and I must needs flatten my nose against the pavement instead of crying, Halt!"

"Never mind," said Felix, "how could you know that it wasn't a real ghost? Come, let us find Diego. I have an idea."

"I warrant thou hast," cried Tortosa admiringly, as he followed Felix.

They soon met Diego and Father Juan Perez. The good Superior's face expressed the deepest concern and anxiety.

"Diego," cried Felix, "bring Perrito to your room, and let him smell of that cupboard, and I'm mistaken if he doesn't track the thief."

"A good idea," said Juan Perez. "Bring the dog at once."

Diego brought Perrito to the room, and when he smelt of the cabinet, he growled and struggled to free himself. Diego released him, and he passed swiftly through the corridors with his nose to the pavement, followed by the party of interested observers.

Emerging at length into an open courtyard at the rear of the convent, the dog crossed it to the opposite wall, where grew a large fig-tree. Here he looked up and whined, and then suddenly plunged into a thick clump of shrubbery and dragged out a white robe in which were wrapped a mask with goggle eyes, and a wig with shaven crown.

It was all very plain. From that ghostly paraphernalia had emerged the cunning Vascoña, who then had scaled the wall by means of the fig-tree and escaped with his booty.

"Let us follow him," cried Felix. "The dog will track him."

"He is far away by this time," said Juan

Perez, "but he must be pursued. Tortosa, arm thyself. Felix can bear the crossbow, and Diego must go in order properly to manage the dog. I will give ye good mules. Saddle up, and be gone. Do not show your faces at La Rabida again without the charts.

I will despatch *alguazils* from Palos to aid ye."

In a short time the three pursuers were mounted and ready to set out. Tortosa had donned his old armor, and bore a long Toledo sword. Felix carried his crossbow and a good supply of arrows. Diego was unarmed.

Perrito quickly found the trail, and they

rode briskly forward. They soon came to a spot in a little wood of pines where the trampled earth showed that Vascoña had tied his horse there while he went to the convent.

The dog now made a long detour, and in a little while struck a road leading away towards the frontier of Portugal.

All day they followed the sagacious animal, who took up the trail swiftly even on the highway. Twice they obtained inforformation from peasants regarding the fugitive. In the afternoon they passed through a town where they again heard news of Vascoña.

Night came, but they rode on by moonlight. Vascoña had so long a start, besides being better mounted, that their only hope lay in unflagging pursuit. For supper they ate bread and cheese that they had brought with them, and drank at springs by the roadside.

They were now entering the mountains, and the road wound through dense woods, or traversed the bare, steep slopes of lofty hills. Towards morning they halted in a grassy spot to rest and feed their mules. Tortosa and Felix threw themselves on the ground and slept heavily, but Diego sat with his back against a tree and held Perrito's leash. He was too anxious to sleep.

In about two hours they resumed their journey in the dusky dawn. They soon came to a vast gorge in the mountains. The road was a narrow shelf cut in a high cliff. Above were rugged precipices; far below was a black river rushing among jagged rocks. A hoarse roar came up from the gulf.

Diego said something about Thermopylæ, but Felix and Tortosa had never heard that celebrated name, and did not understand what he was talking about.

After passing the gorge, they reached, late in the forenoon, a little mountain hamlet. Inquiring of the rough and surly inhabitants, they learned that a man answering the description of Vascoña had spent the night there, and had departed early in the morning. Therefore he was still far in advance of them.

Tortosa and the boys pushed on again,

determined to continue the pursuit even to the gates of Lisbon, if necessary.

About three miles beyond the hamlet, as they were riding through a wild mountain pass, Perrito paused, and seemed for a moment at fault.

Hastening up, they saw that the soft earth was marked with numerous hoof tracks, which finally led in a distinct trail up the side of the densely wooded mountain.

While they were exchanging surmises about this, they were surprised and startled to see the dog move forward and take the trail up the mountain.

"The Portuguese thief has met a squad of his friends, sure," growled Tortosa seriously.

"Follow — follow!" cried Felix. "We must see where they have gone."

They followed Perrito up the dizzy trail, turning in sharp zigzags back and forth. Through rifts in the thick foliage of the woods they saw below them a vast mountain panorama.

After climbing in this way for an hour, they reached open woods, where the ground

was less rugged. In half an hour more they suddenly found themselves in the vicinity of the people they had been pursuing.

At that place the precipitous hillside above them descended abruptly to the more level land. Built against the steep slope was a small stone hut, with a roof of thick thatch. Gathered before this hut were a dozen ill-looking fellows, and among them they easily distinguished the more graceful form of Vascoña. A number of horses and mules were tied to trees near by.

Diego trembled as he saw his father's charts unrolled in the hands of a tall, ugly man, whose big ears stood out almost straight from his head. He sprang from his mule and secured Perrito by his leash.

Even Tortosa recoiled at sight of this assemblage.

"Zooks! They are too many for us," he grumbled.

But it was too late to retreat, for the strangers had seen them, and instantly sprang to their arms. Crossbows were displayed, and the man with the charts levelled a huge arquebuse, like a small cannon. But the deadly volley was withheld when they perceived the small numbers of the approaching party.

"Come up,— come up!" shouted the man with the arquebuse, who was evidently the leader. "Quick, or we'll shoot!"

"We must take the bull by the horns, boys," said Tortosa coolly, and at once led the way forward to the band of ruffians.

Vascoña looked a little surprised as they rode up, but he remained cool and silent. Something in the appearance of the gang set Tortosa to thinking. He noticed that one of the men had Vascoña's sword, and he at once made a very shrewd guess how the matter stood. As he supposed, the strangers were *contrabandistas*, or smugglers. They had met Vascoña and captured him, and were now trying to ascertain the value of their prize.

"Who are you? What do you want?" asked the chief, in a surly tone, as he noted the plain appearance of the newcomers and their tired mules.

"Caballéro," replied Tortosa, in a big voice, "we are in pursuit of that man yonder, in order to recover those charts, which he stole night before last from the convent of La Rabida at Palos."

"Stole!" cried Vascoña, stepping forward angrily.

"That's what we call it in Andalusia," replied Tortosa coolly.

"'Tis false," said Vascoña, turning to the chief. "What I have just told you is the truth. The king of Portugal sent me to Spain to procure these charts. I had fulfilled my commission and was returning to Lisbon when you met me."

"Procure!" echoed Tortosa, indignantly. "Is that thy fine word for midnight robbery?"

The *contrabandistas* had now gathered about to hear the dispute.

"The maps belong to a sea captain named Christopher Columbus, and this is his boy here beside me," continued Tortosa. "The king and queen of Spain are going to give Señor Columbus a fleet of ships, and he is going to discover a country he knows about, where even the sands on the beach are of pure gold, and diamonds hang on the trees like dew."

This glittering announcement made a sensation among the smugglers, and they listened with breathless interest.

"Señor," said Vascoña, haughtily, to the chief, "you can see that these are but shabby fellows. Is it probable that these valuable charts belong to them or their friends? I am a trusted agent of the king of Portugal, and I am to be believed. Give me my charts, and let me resume my journey, and you shall receive one thousand ducats. Beware how you detain me, and incur the anger of King John."

This made another sensation. But the chief replied, —

"Your threats don't frighten us. But what security can we have that the money will be paid?"

"Accompany me to the vicinity of Beja, or any other Portuguese city, and keep the charts in your hands until you receive the money," replied Vascoña.

Diego, who was very pale, had been whispering eagerly to Tortosa.

"Caballéro," spoke out the old soldier loudly, addressing the chief, "thou canst see that this Portuguese, in spite of his fine words, is a rogue. Return the charts to us, and thou shalt receive two thousand ducats from the queen of Castile. Go with us to the neighborhood of Palos, and keep the charts until the money is thine."

"Two thousand ducats!" sneered Vascoña. "Señor, these peasants could not raise two thousand maravedis. This boy's father is a crack-brained enthusiast of whom I bought one or two maps. He has probably sent these three scamps to waylay and rob me. As for his being recognized by the queen of Castile, it is simply ridiculous. Come, I must go at once. You shall receive three thousand ducats."

"Caballéro," cried Tortosa, "whatever he offers, the queen of Castile will pay thee more. Return with us as far as thou canst, and assure thyself that I speak the truth."

"Boy," said the puzzled chief to Diego, "has thy father a commission from the queen of Castile?"

"Say, *Yes, yes!*" whispered Tortoso anxiously.

"No, Señor," replied Diego, calmly, while Tortosa uttered a suppressed groan. "But her Highness has summoned my father to Court, and as soon as the war in Granada is ended, he will receive his commission and his ships."

"I believe thou speakest honestly," said the chief, slapping his thigh.

"Señor, do not be deceived by these vulgar boors," cried Vascoña.

"We will see about that," said the chief. "Boy, if these charts belong to thy father, thou canst tell me the titles. Repeat them."

Diego repeated the titles.

"Thou hast answered correctly," cried the chief. "Now, tell me more of thy father's plans, and of that rich country he is going to discover."

"Let me take the charts," said Diego, stepping forward with sparkling eyes, "and I will gladly explain them to you."

The chief gave him the roll, and all the *contrabandistas* gathered around him to listen.

As Columbus before the august assembly at Salamanca explained his sublime beliefs and plans to the learned men of Spain, so did his son, in that wild scene, explain them to the rude men about him. And the wise doctors did not listen with more attention than the ignorant smugglers.

And Diego was kindled with his father's enthusiasm as he proceeded with his demonstrations. His finger swiftly traced parallels and meridians on the charts, and his words poured forth rapidly and triumphantly.

"Marvellous! Wonderful!" murmured the smugglers admiringly.

In the midst of his earnest recital, Diego was startled to see, behind the men, a woman gazing at him with rapt attention. The ragged shawl which was drawn over her head had slipped from her relaxed fingers, and her black hair fell down on each side of her white and haggard face. Her expression was mournful. Her eyes were large and very sad.

So surprised was Diego at seeing this melancholy figure, that he lost the thread of his discourse, and paused.

Then the chief said, —

"Thy father must be a bold captain and a learned man, and thou art a bright boy to learn all this. Now, I believe thy comrade's story. The charts belong to thy father without doubt."

"Señor," said Vascoña, "I have something to tell you privately. Step aside with me."

He drew the chief aside and spoke earnestly in a low tone, while Tortosa and the boys looked on anxiously. They observed that the chief nodded his head and seemed deeply impressed. Presently they returned, and Vascoña could not repress a smile of triumph.

"Boy," said the chief, "according to thy own story thy father has not yet received his commission from the queen, nor will he until the war in Granada is at an end. Methinks, then, thy chance of redeeming the charts is small, and may be long delayed, while this cavalier offers us the money at once. We must accept the best offer; but if the charts really belong to thy father, and he has influence with the queen, let him negotiate with the king of Portugal regarding them."

"Caballéro," roared Tortosa, "if the king of Portugal secures these charts, they are forever lost to their rightful owner, the good Señor Columbus. I assure thee that the queen of Castile will pay thee instantly more than will the Portuguese king."

The chief seemed perplexed. Suddenly the woman, who had been listening intently, stepped forward and spoke a few vehement sentences to him in favor of Diego. The ruffian repulsed her angrily; but at once a noisy and violent dispute arose among the smugglers, some being in favor of Vascoña, and some advocating Diego's cause. At last the chief, raising his voice above the hubbub, shouted,—

"I will consider this matter to-night, and to-morrow will give my decision."

He turned abruptly, and pushing open the massive wooden door of the hut, entered, taking the charts with him. The woman followed him, slowly and listlessly.

Some of the *contrabandistas* now began to unsaddle the horses and mules, while others built a large fire, and put pieces of goat's flesh on spits to roast for the evening meal.

Vascoña, Tortosa, and the boys were left entirely at liberty, as the smugglers knew that their anxiety for the charts would insure their stay.

Tortosa, Diego, and Felix led their mules a little way down the hill, and tied them to trees where they could nibble grass. Perrito, also, was tied up, so that he might not get into trouble.

When night came on, they joined the smugglers at their rude meal of goat's meat, bread, and cheese, and listened to the conversation of the rough men, from which they gathered that theirs was a life whose toil and hardship far exceeded that of more honest occupations.

At last, one by one, the smugglers threw themselves upon the earth to sleep. The chief retired again to the hut, where he had the charts safely secured, and Felix heard him bar the heavy door.

Tortosa and the boys left the fire and lay down under a low, thick pine-tree, not far from their mules. Tortosa and Diego soon fell asleep, but Felix remained alert and watchful. Several hours passed. The fire died down to coals. The moon rose, strewing patches of white light among the deep shadows of the woods. Then Felix rose also, and stole up the hill. He made a circuit around the sleeping smugglers, and approached the hut from the side. He had resolved to secure the charts, if possible, and escape with them.

As he crouched behind a bush hardly twenty feet from the building, he heard a slight noise, as if the door was being unbarred. In a moment the door opened slowly, and the strange woman stepped out. After a cautious glance about her, she glided away in the shadows, her dress almost brushing Felix as he lay behind the bush. She disappeared among the trees.

Felix turned his attention to the hut again. The woman had closed the door, but it was unfastened, and, with his usual promptness, he lost no time in entering.

All was dark inside, but from a corner he heard the heavy breathing of the sleeping smuggler. Felix at once began a cautious search for the charts. Inch by inch he moved about the hut, feeling everywhere. Several times he paused, as a slight movement led him to think that the chief was awaking.

He could not find the maps, and his courage began to fail. But again he began a circuit of the room, even passing his hands about the smuggler, who was lying on the earth-floor wrapped in goatskins. At that critical moment, the door swung open noiselessly, and the woman stepped in.

Felix shrank down in a corner and wished himself at home. He did not give way to a panic, however, but resolved to remain quiet until he had a chance to slip out and escape, or even to resume his search. He noted that the woman had not bolted the door again.

But her actions puzzled him. She moved so quietly that he could hardly tell where she was, but it suddenly flashed upon him that she, too, was searching the hut. Had she seen him enter? Was she searching for him?

Suddenly an icy hand touched his face, and he almost cried out with terror. He rose, but the hand covered his mouth, and the woman whispered, —

"Don't speak. Listen to me. Return to your friends at once. They are waiting for you."

She drew him to the door and he slipped out quickly. It was instantly shut and fastened. He stole down the hill, and found Tortosa and Diego, with the mules saddled, anxiously watching for him.

Diego had met with a singular adventure. He had sunk into a deep sleep, and dreamed that his dead mother came and bent down and kissed him. Then he awoke, and lo! a dark figure knelt beside him in the moonlight. He thought it was an apparition, and uttered a silent prayer.

But the figure bent down and whispered, —

"Awake, thou must go at once. I have brought thee thy charts, for I know they are thine. To-morrow he would have given them to the Portuguese. Awaken thy companion and hasten away."

Diego recognized the strange woman. She thrust the roll of charts into his hands. His heart swelled with joy and gratitude.

"Oh, Señora," he replied, taking the woman's hand, "how can we ever thank thee, — my father and I!"

She was silent, but presently he knew that she was weeping. At last she said, wildly and mournfully, —

"I once had a little son, fair and beautiful like thee, but he is in heaven. Oh, shall I ever see him again? Perhaps I shall die — soon. Pray for me, oh, pray for me!"

She arose, sobbing, and hurried away.

Diego's eyes were full of tears of sympathy. He did not then realize that there was a dire significance in her words.

He sprang up and awoke Tortosa, who was snoring hideously, for the old soldier was very tired. Then they were astonished to discover that Felix was gone. However, they saddled the mules and prepared for a start, and in a few minutes Felix came hurrying down to them, breathing very fast and looking surprised and scared. In a few words Diego told him of the recovery of the charts.

They mounted and stole away, followed by the faithful Perrito. It was with difficulty that they found their way down the steep trail, and they often feared that the clatter of the mule's hoofs on the rocks would be heard by the smugglers. Once they went astray, and were in terror lest morning should find them lost in the neighborhood of their enemies.

To their great joy they at last reached the road and set out with all possible speed for home. But morning had dawned before they passed through the little mountain hamlet. Several rough men on the street looked at them suspiciously, but did not molest them.

After leaving the village, the road passed around the head of a ravine, and then returned along the vast flank of the mountain. At the latter point, as they were riding quietly along, a tremendous report came from the other side of the ravine, where the road left the hamlet. There was a strange humming sound in the air around them.

"What's that?" cried Diego, startled.

"Ha, ha!" laughed Tortosa grimly, "I have heard that sound before. Ride, boys, ride as fast as you can."

Looking across the ravine, they saw the whole party of smugglers in swift pursuit, headed by Vascoña and the chief, who had just fired his arquebuse.

Tortosa and the boys urged their mules on, but the Superior's animals were unused to long and severe journeys, and they were already tired out. It was plain that they would be overtaken very quickly.

They had now entered the vast and precipitous gorge, and, looking back as they wound around the gigantic cliffs, they saw the smugglers riding fast and gaining on them at every step.

Suddenly Felix pulled up, and jumped from his mule. Diego, who was in a great panic, rode on at full speed, but Tortosa, with soldierly instinct, halted to see what was the matter.

"They will catch us at this rate, Tortosa." shouted Felix. "I am going to blockade

the road; but you ride on with Diego and guard the charts."

Tortosa hesitated. He did not like the plan.

"Ride on! ride on!" yelled Felix, who had sprung upon the steep bank and was furiously rolling huge rocks down into the road. "You can't do any good here. Guard Diego and the charts!"

THE PURSUIT. 105

Tortosa was accustomed to obey orders. He rode on, and left the courageous boy at his task.

Having rolled down all the available rocks, Felix took a small axe that hung at his saddle-bow, and chopped two or three young pines so that they fell down across the road, though still hanging to the stumps.

He now heard the clatter of the smugglers' horses near at hand. His barrier, if not defended, could be quickly removed. He led his mule behind a projecting point of rock  which would partially protect him from shots. Then he seized his crossbow and placed an arrow on the string, just as the pursuers appeared around the nearest turn, and rode down upon his rude barricade.

CHAPTER VI.

THE SAILING OF THE FLEET.

TORTOSA found it difficult to overtake Diego, who was riding like the Wild Huntsman. In less than half an hour they galloped into a small town, where everybody ran out of doors to see what was the matter.

Tortosa instantly tried to drum up recruits to ride back with him and rescue Felix. He persuaded a few men to go. Falstaff's ragged regiment was not more grotesque than they. As the old soldier reviewed them with a gloomy countenance, he was delighted to see four well-armed and well-mounted *alguazils* ride up. They had been sent from Palos by Father Juan Perez.

Leaving Diego at the house of the village priest, with the precious charts in his care, Tortosa and his men returned at full speed to the assistance of Felix. Perrito was eager to go with them, and bounded away joyfully when his master gave him permission.

"Find Felix, boy, find Felix!" cried Diego to the dog.

When they entered the gorge they found it deserted. The barricade had been partially removed, and they saw that horsemen had passed through. They shouted to Felix, but there was no answer. The only sounds to be heard were the mournful sough of the wind in the pines, and the sullen roar of the vexed river far below.

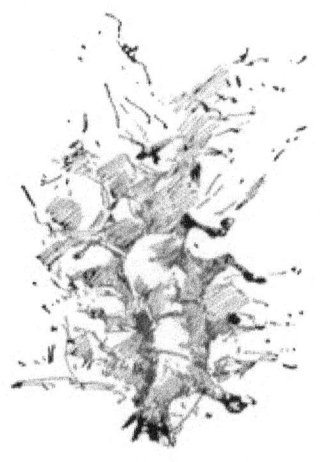

Suddenly one of the *alguazils* uttered a word of alarm, and pointed over the precipice. They all looked and saw the body of a saddled mule lying among the rocks. Tortosa gazed at it long and earnestly.

"It is Felix's mule!" he said. "Where is my brave boy?" He sat down on a rock and covered his face, and uttered grievous lamentations, and reproached himself for permitting Felix to stay behind.

There was no way of descending into the abyss, and though they looked long and anxiously, they saw no traces of the mule's rider. After extending their search to the farther end of the gorge, they sadly returned to the town. Before they arrived, they noticed that Perrito had disappeared, but none could tell where he had left them.

Diego's grief was very sharp at the loss of Felix, whom he had grown to love as a brother. Although the tailor's boy was wholly uneducated in books, yet his prompt, alert, courageous spirit had won the admiration of Diego, who was a student, and more given to gentle thought than decisive action.

So the party returned very sadly to Palos. At the convent they found the physician, Garcia Fernandez, in company with Father Juan Perez. Their joy at the recovery of the charts was overshadowed by sorrow at the uncertain fate of Felix.

"It is probable that he has perished at the hands of those revengeful men," said Juan Perez. "If so, he has met a hero's death. Such are worthy of Paradise."

THE SAILING OF THE FLEET.

"I will not believe that the boy is dead," cried Garcia Fernandez. "He has escaped them in some way, depend upon it." He looked around fiercely, as if defying any one to differ with him, but he saw sad eyes and gloomy faces wherever he looked. So, concealing a groan behind a cough, he hastily departed from the convent.

The next day the physician entered the shop of Ignacio Diaz, with a frowning, important air. The tailor met him with a lugubrious countenance, for one of the brothers of the convent had just informed him of the probable death of Felix, and Ignacio Diaz saw the hitherto possible one hundred ducats fading away forever.

"Alas! my poor Felix is dead, Señor Fernandez," he wailed. "Such a fine boy, too. So careful, so skilful, so industrious,—and now he is gone—"

"Silence!" cried the physician furiously. "He is *not* dead, I tell you. I said I would pay you for his time until he returned, and I keep my word. Here is the money for the next three months. He is alive, do you hear?" And the despotic, kind-hearted doctor blustered out of the shop, having thus healed the tailor's broken heart.

Two or three months passed, but nothing was heard of Felix or Perrito. Diego grieved deeply, and devoted himself to his studies in order, if possible, to soothe the sharp sting of his sorrow. Even the joyful tidings that Queen Isabella had at last resolved to undertake his father's grand enterprise could not dispel his melancholy. The results of overstudy and lack of exercise were soon apparent. Diego became ill.

Mingled with this grief, he constantly felt deep pity for the strange lady of the mountains. He never forgot her, and in the bright morning or in the solemn night he always remembered her in his prayers. A shadowy fear ever haunted him that she had suffered for her good deed.

One pleasant evening in May, Tortosa hurried into Diego's chamber, where the boy, though dressed, was lying listlessly on his bed, and cried, —

"Thy father has come, Diego. There's a hubbub at the gate, I can tell thee. Come, he is asking for thee. The queen has given him ships, and he is going to sail in three weeks."

Diego sprang up with new energy and ran out to the garden, while Tortosa followed more slowly, muttering to himself,—

"Who would have thought that the world is round! Who knows whether he is on top or underneath? Zooks! when I have a headache after this, I'll know the reason for it!"

At the end of the cloister Diego saw a group of monks, and among them the white head and noble figure of his father. The next moment Columbus saw him, and came striding swiftly down the cloister, and Diego was soon warmly clasped in his arms. "My son," said his father tenderly, "I grieve to see thee so thin and pale. Thou must get well quickly. If I should lose thee, of what value would be the triumph I have gained?"

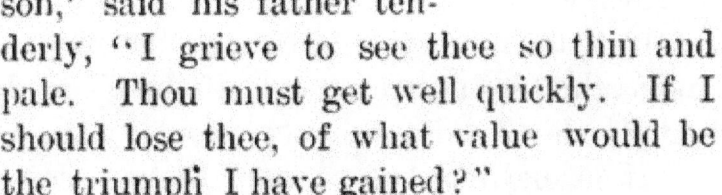

"I cannot forget Felix, father," said Diego mournfully.

"He has performed for us an inestimable service," said Columbus. "Before I depart, I will have a thorough search made for him. Let us trust that he may be restored to us. Come, sit on this bench by the fountain, and I will tell thee of my success."

So they sat down in the pleasant twilight, and Columbus told of the surrender of Granada by Mohammed Boabdil, the last of the Moorish kings, and how the royal standard of Spain was unfurled on the gorgeous towers of the Alhambra.

He told of the refusal of the Court authorities at first to admit his high claims to be appointed admiral and viceroy of all the countries he might discover, and of his departure from Court with the determination to apply to France; and of his recall by a royal courier, ere he had rode three leagues, with the tidings that the queen had resolved to agree to his conditions and to undertake his enterprise, even if she pledged her jewels to raise the necessary funds.

"It is eighteen years ago, Diego," continued Columbus, "since I began this undertaking, and I thank heaven that I have been

enabled to persevere. It is a glorious thing never to despair, no matter how great are the disappointments and misfortunes that come to us."

"And are you really to have the ships?" cried Diego.

"I have the royal order to the authorities of Palos, requiring them to furnish me two caravels, fully manned and equipped for sea, within ten days. I intend to fit out a third vessel myself, with the assistance of Señor Pinzon. I shall have the royal orders read to-morrow in Palos, and in less than a month I expect to sail."

"It seems like a dream," said Diego. "But what am I to do? Can I go with you, father?"

"No, my son. I have something better for thee than that. Read this letter patent, signed as you see by her Highness Queen Isabella. It concerns thee, and will assure thee that thou art not dreaming."

Diego read the document, which appointed him page to Prince Juan, the heir apparent to the Spanish throne. This was a very high honor, and included an allowance for his support. Diego was surprised and delighted; but the next moment he became grave as he thought of the approaching separation from his father.

"Thou shalt remain here until I sail," said Columbus. "Then Father Juan Perez will conduct thee to Cordova, where thou must enter school."

The next day Columbus, accompanied by Father Juan Perez, Garcia Fernandez, and Martin Alonzo Pinzon, repaired to the church of St. George in Palos, where the *alcalde*, or magistrate, the *regidores*, or councilmen, and the *alguazils*, or constables, and the chief inhabitants had been summoned to meet him.

When the notary public read the royal order in the porch of the church, and the officials and the people began to realize the nature of the voyage about to be undertaken, there was great consternation. If, at the present day, some daring explorer should construct a sky-ship in which he proposed to abandon the earth, and should demand men to accompany him, probably there would be a similar disturbance.

Before night the entire town was in an uproar. On the wharves, in the countinghouses, the courts, and the shops, and in every dwelling, a thousand voluble tongues were busy discussing the extraordinary voyage and its probable consequences. It was everywhere condemned as a reckless sacrifice of ships and lives.

The only man in town who was entirely satisfied was the tailor, Ignacio Diaz. Columbus had visited his shop that day and given him an order for a rich suit of scarlet cloth embroidered with gold. As the tailor counted up his probable profit, his smile broadened, and he did not heed the sailors in the street, who were talking loudly and angrily about the crazy foreigner, Christopher Columbus, while their wives were weeping near by.

Columbus found his departure delayed. Neither ships nor men could be obtained. At last further orders were issued by Ferdinand and Isabella, and an officer of the royal household was sent to see that they were obeyed.

But still little progress was made until Martin Alonzo Pinzon and his brother engaged to furnish a ship and sail on the voyage. Two other ships were pressed into the service, and their owners and crews compelled to serve on board.

One of these vessels was the fleet *Pinta*,

that Felix had so often admired as she sailed up the river. Her owner, Gomez Rascon, was furious, and among his townsmen made many threats, and did all he could to delay the expedition.

All this consumed time, and two months elapsed. Columbus had been so engrossed with severe and vexatious labors that he had not yet instituted a thorough search for Felix.

One evening in July, Diego was walking on the street at Palos with his father, having been to inspect the ships, when they met a tall, ugly man, who saluted Columbus as he passed. His big ears stuck out almost straight from his head. Diego caught his father's arm. He was very pale.

"Father, that is the chief of the *contrabandistas* who had the charts!"

"Is it possible?" said Columbus, looking after the man. "He enlisted in my service a month ago. I shall question him at once and find out what became of Felix."

He spoke to an *alguazil*, and soon after the former chief of the *contrabandistas* was arrested and brought before Columbus at the office of the *alcalde*. He was very cool and unconcerned.

"Don Christopher Columbus," he said, "I know why I am brought here. I recognize your son, who visited me in the mountains, and of course he could not fail to recognize me. But I beg to remind you that by the terms of my enlistment, as with all your sailors, I am exempt from criminal processes during the voyage and for two months after my return."

"It is true," replied Columbus, "thou art exempt from criminal prosecution. But we are very anxious to know the fate of the boy who barricaded the road while his companions escaped."

"Did he never return?" asked the man, with genuine surprise.

"He never returned," replied Columbus.

"Tell us truthfully what thou knowest concerning him."

"I can tell you little more than you know, Señor," said the chief. "We were in a rage at the loss of the charts. I must have slept like a pig. The Portuguese rogue was angry, too, and we made the dirt fly.

"We rode around a turn of the road and ran on to a neat little barricade. The boy let fly an arrow. It pinned a man to his mule by the leg. The mule kicked high, and nearly knocked some of us over the edge.

"We went back a little, and some of the men climbed up the cliff so as to get around and cut off the man and boys, for we thought at first that they were all there.

"We shot arrows at the barricade. I saw the boy's mule partly behind a rock, and fired my arquebuse. The beast reared and fell over the precipice.

"Just then the Portuguese, Vascoña, left us and rode toward the barricade. We thought he was only reconnoitring, until he clapped spurs to his fine beast and galloped down the road. The boy shot at him — missed — and the next instant Vascoña leaped his horse over the barricade.

"We all mounted and rode down, making a joyous hullabaloo, like fools. Our animals couldn't jump the barricade. It was a hard thing to do. And by the time we had torn it down so as to pass, we saw Vascoña afar off, riding like the wind, with the boy held before him on the saddle.

"We chased for a while, but we lost him, and the others too. So we went back like whipped dogs, snarling at one another.

"I don't know what became of Vascoña or the boy. If the little rogue juggled him out of the charts, very likely he tossed him over the cliff, and went back to Portugal."

Columbus and Diego received very little comfort from the ruffian's narrative. They were both sad and silent. At length Columbus asked,—

"Is this the truth?"

The man uttered imprecations to attest his veracity.

"Why did you enlist in this expedition?" inquired Columbus.

"Ah," said the chief, with a leer, "I want to see those sands of gold, and the diamonds hanging on the trees like dew."

Columbus sighed, and said no more.

Another thought now came to Diego. A deep anxiety came over him to hear tidings of the strange lady who had been so kind to him. He spoke timidly to the smuggler, —

"Where is the lady whom we saw in the mountains, — your wife, was she not? Is she quite well?"

For an instant the man darted at him a strange, fierce, evil look. Then he dropped his gaze, and replied, with seeming sorrow, —

"Alas! she is dead."

Diego was shocked. A hideous fear that he dared not utter even to himself overcame him. That night he prayed for his dead benefactress, in grief and tears.

The next day Columbus sent out three *alguazils* with orders to make a thorough search for Felix.

After a thousand difficulties and delays, the fleet was at last ready to sail. Ignacio Diaz had finished the suit of scarlet and gold, and it was really a very fine affair. The tailor was heard on several occasions to express his sorrow that so good a customer as Don Christopher Columbus should persist in sailing away into unknown regions, where he would surely be boiled alive in tropic seas, or swallowed up by huge monsters that lurked on the borders of the world, or sucked over the edge of a vast abyss, like a bug over a cataract.

"Good-by to Don Christopher and his beautiful new suit," said Ignacio Diaz to his wife, nodding his head solemnly.

"But it is paid for, Diaz," cried his wife sharply.

"Yes, my love, it is paid for," replied the tailor, with a sweet smile of resignation.

On the second of August, Columbus, his officers, and crew, made solemn preparations for their departure, observing all the religious rites which were deemed to be due to so serious an occasion. The fleet was anchored at the sand bar, near the mouth of the Tinto, fully equipped and ready to sail.

It was a sad night in Palos, for the people generally believed that all who were

THE SAILING OF THE FLEET.

about to sail on the expedition were surely doomed to death. And while there was weeping on shore, as the inhabitants bade their relatives and friends farewell, two men in the darkness were busy tampering with the rudder of the *Pinta*. One of them was Gomez Rascon, who wished to disable his ship so that she might be left behind. The other was the *contrabandista*, who had easily been hired, for a few pieces of silver, to assist in the treacherous deed.

In the early morning hours, Columbus was at the convent, where he had been engaged in solemn conference with Father Juan Perez, and had taken affectionate leave of Diego. Then, accompanied by the Superior, Diego, Tortosa, and several monks, he set out for the landing in the dim light of dawn.

"Diego," said Tortosa, in a low tone, as they walked along, "I am very ignorant. I know nothing of the earth and sea. Yet, if I were able, I would follow thy father fearlessly, believing in his knowledge. When I was a soldier, I obeyed every order without question, trusting in the skilful plans of my officers, no matter how desperate the service appeared. And dost thou not believe, Diego, that in this enterprise thy father is but fearlessly obeying the orders of God, given him in mysterious ways?"

Before Diego could reply, the quick tramp of horses' feet was heard, and three men overtook them. They were the *alguazils* that Columbus had sent to search for Felix. They looked pale and jaded.

"Have ye found the lad?" asked Columbus, as they drew near.

"We found no trace of him, Señor," replied the men gloomily.

Columbus walked on, repeating in a low voice words of resignation, to which Father Juan Perez responded.

In a little while they reached the landing, where a large crowd had sorrowfully assembled to witness the departure of the fleet. A last farewell to Diego and his friends, and Columbus entered his boat and went on board the *Santa Maria*, where from the masthead his admiral's flag was floating on the breeze. The east was gorgeous with the coming sun. The anchors were raised, the sails were set, and, amid doleful lamentations from the shore, the fleet departed on its long and mysterious voyage.

Columbus shaped his course for the Canary Islands, thence intending to sail due west. Three days after leaving Palos, the results of Gomez Rascon's plot became apparent. The *Pinta's* rudder was found to be broken and unshipped, and only the excellent seamanship of Pinzon, her commander, enabled her to reach the Canaries in her crippled condition.

The fleet remained at the islands three weeks. Columbus at first endeavored to find a vessel to replace the *Pinta*, but, not succeeding, he had a new rudder made.

The repairs were completed at last, and the fleet anchored at the island of Gomera to take in wood, water, and provisions.

One evening when the sailors had ceased their labors for the day, Columbus stood on the lofty stern of the *Santa Maria* gazing at the sky in the northeast, which was lurid with the eruption of the volcano of Teneriffe.

Presently his attention was drawn to a

small caravel, which came swiftly gliding in from sea. As she passed astern of the *Santa Maria*, Columbus saw a boy on the high forecastle gazing intently at him. He held a crossbow in his hand, and a dog stood beside him looking up as eagerly as his master. Then the dog began to utter plaintive bays.

The caravel came to anchor, and a boat was instantly lowered. The boy and the dog sprang in, the oarsmen pulled away vigorously, and were soon alongside of the *Santa Maria*. The boy came on deck, followed by his dog, and, to the questions of the officers, earnestly demanded to be taken to Columbus. He was conducted aft, and when the Admiral saw him, he cried, with astonishment, —

"Felix!—and Perrito!" for the dog was leaping upon him joyfully.

"Señor Columbus," said Felix seriously, "I come to inform you that three armed Portuguese caravels, under the command of Don Juan Vascoña, are cruising in the vicinity of the island of Ferro with the intention of attacking you."

"How dost thou know this?" asked Columbus.

"I saw them when I left Ferro in that caravel, whose captain I promised one hundred ducats if he would bring me to you," replied Felix.

"He shall be paid at once," said Columbus. "Thy information is valuable. And when I am at leisure I wish to learn how thou camest here, so far from Spain."

He then gave orders for the boats immediately to resume the work of getting the stores aboard. The cannon and other arms were prepared for instant use. All night the work went on by the light of the gigantic torch of Teneriffe.

CHAPTER VII.

THE NEW WORLD.

EARLY the next morning the fleet set sail from Gomera. At the earnest request of Felix, Columbus had permitted him to join the expedition, and, of course, Perrito went also. They hoped soon to be far be-

yond the pursuit of the Portuguese squadron, but, to their great disappointment, a dead calm suddenly fell, and left their sails idly hanging at the mast. They apprehensively scanned the horizon for Vascoña's fleet, and the sailors whistled for a breeze, and called out, piously, —

"*Blow,
San Antonio!*"

Columbus exhibited his usual supreme patience at this trying mischance. He summoned Felix to the cabin, and kindly asked him to give an account of his movements and adventures since Tortosa and Diego left him at the barricade. The boy willingly complied, and his narrative was substantially as follows : —

When Vascoña made his sudden charge in the gorge, Felix, who had been somewhat appalled at the effect of his first shot, hastily let fly an arrow, which flew wide of the mark, and the next moment Vascoña, with a shout, had leaped the barricade.

Felix retreated, trying to adjust his bow for another shot, but the cavalier rode down upon him, laughing, and, bending down, caught his arm and drew him upon the horse. Then he galloped away down the road at a good pace, while the *contrabandistas* followed, hallooing loudly.

"Felix," said Vascoña, "if those rogues catch thee, thou art a dead boy."

Felix did not answer.

"They are desperate men and very angry," continued Vascoña. "See, they are tearing down thy barricade. If I should set thee afoot now, they would be upon thee in five minutes. On one condition I will bear thee away and save thy life. Thou must aid me to regain the charts, and I will pay to thee one thousand ducats. Thou canst rejoin thy companions, and take the charts stealthily, and give them to me. If thou fearest discovery, I will take thee to Portugal and find thee an honorable place. Thou shalt no longer be a wretched tailor."

"Honorable!" cried Felix indignantly. "No place would ever be honorable to me again if I should do such a thing,— not even my grave!"

"Dost thou refuse, stupid?" said Vascoña fiercely.

"Yes," returned Felix, though he was really very much frightened.

"Then stay, and settle thy score with those mountain ruffians," cried Vascoña, pushing him roughly to the ground. The cavalier then clapped spurs to his horse and darted away a few yards, but suddenly pulled up and wheeled about as if to try Felix once more. But the boy had not waited for the test. He was springing up the steep mountain-side with the hope of eluding the *contrabandistas*, who had passed the barricade, and were now galloping down the road.

"Little fool!" growled Vascoña, and in a moment his powerful horse had overtaken Felix, and he was again lifted to the saddle. "They would snare thee like a young rabbit, and show thee no more mercy," laughed the cavalier. "I will save thy life in spite of thee." And as he spoke he was recklessly thundering down the mountain road at prodigious speed.

Vascoña travelled rapidly into Portugal, compelling Felix to go with him. He jestingly called him his prisoner, but really he had taken a great fancy to the boy.

They had not gone far before Perrito overtook them, having faithfully obeyed Diego's orders to find Felix. Vascoña, who had an antipathy to the dog, would have killed him, but yielded to the boy's entreaties for his life. He stipulated, however, that Felix should lead Perrito with him, so that he might not be used to track them.

One day Vascoña asked him how they had recovered the charts. Felix answered truthfully, and the cavalier became very grave and thoughtful.

When they arrived at Lisbon, Felix was treated very kindly, and was given an agreeable position in Vascoña's household. But the people with whom he was brought in contact were gay, fashionable, and dissipated, and Felix became insensibly corrupted by them. He forgot Palos and his old friends in a round of gay spectacles and frivolous diversions. He was making a brilliant start on the road to ruin.

But Felix was suddenly brought to his senses. He had for a while observed that his patron was engaged in some important business, and one day certain of his associates casually mentioned that Vascoña was to take command of a fleet of ships about to sail for the Canary Islands, to intercept and capture a Spanish adventurer named Columbus!

The brave, honest spirit of Felix revived within him. He was seriously troubled between his obligations to Vascoña, and his duty to Columbus. But his sense of the injustice and iniquity of Vascoña's mission, and his high estimation of Columbus, at length brought him to a decision. Leaving behind him all the rich clothing and trinkets given him by Vascoña, he took Perrito and his crossbow, and, dressed in his old, ragged suit, secretly took passage on a caravel bound for the Canary Islands. After many minor adventures, he at last reached Columbus and gave him warning.

"Thou hast done well, Felix," said Columbus. "Not every one could or would abandon a life of luxury and ease for poverty, hardship, and an uncertain fate, in the effort to do right. We are now embarked in an enterprise from which, I trust, will come honor and riches. Ask of me, Felix, whatever thou wilt, and, if it be

possible, I will give it thee at the termination of this voyage."

Columbus smiled kindly and waited to hear his wish, encouraging him to ask for whatever would please him most. Suddenly Felix looked up and asked earnestly, —

"Señor, do you think it would be possible for me to learn to read?"

"To read!" cried Columbus, surprised. "Thou canst easily learn."

"If you would teach me," murmured Felix; "but no! it is asking too much."

"Felix," said Columbus gently, "I will gladly teach thee to read. Let us begin now, and afterward we will speak again of the reward which thou shalt receive."

"That will be a reward beyond my deserving," cried Felix. "To be a learned man, — to know how to read!"

So while his ships lay motionless on a glassy sea, in proximity to an enemy, Columbus calmly gave Felix his first lesson in letters.

In three days a fresh breeze sprang up as the sun rose on a Sunday morning. Far away towered the mountains of Ferro, and on the horizon under the sun three white specks gleamed. They were the Portuguese caravels. But the ships of Columbus spread their wings and sped away into the west, and Vascoña was baffled once more.

Day after day the ships sailed on far into

the mysterious solitudes of the ocean. A strange, steady breeze wafted them along. It was the now familiar trade-wind.

The compass, upon which they had relied, began to act strangely, and the needle no longer pointed directly to the north.

The pilots were puzzled, and the ignorant sailors appalled, and only the wise explanations of Columbus regarding the variation calmed their fears for the time.

Still the mystical breeze blew them on, and they feared that they could never return against that ceaseless current of air.

The sea was smooth, and soon they beheld it covered with weeds, and they imagined that the ships were about to run aground in shallow, shoreless, torrid waters where all would miserably perish. But Columbus sounded the sea and found no bottom.

Weeks passed, and only the level ocean and the arching sky met their eager eyes. They seemed to be carried down a vast watery incline, who could tell where? Perhaps into the depths of a terrible abyss full of enormous whirlpools, or even over the very edge of the world, whence they would plunge into space!

These vague terrors of the sailors led to murmurings and mutiny. Foremost among the disaffected was the *contrabandista*, who had lost all hope of seeing the sands of gold and the diamonds hanging on the trees like dew. His only desire was to get back to Spain, and he incited the sailors to rebel and force Columbus to return.

One night Felix, happening to enter the forecastle, overheard the ruffian urging some of the sailors to join him in throwing Columbus overboard in the night. He argued that it would be regarded as an accident, and that the whole fleet would rejoice at the opportunity to abandon the mad voyage and return to Spain.

Felix at once warned Columbus of his danger, and on the following day the

Admiral addressed his crew, using explanations, promises, or threats, according to the different characters with whom he had to deal. The *contrabandista* and others he sternly menaced with extreme penalties if they attempted any treasonable act.

Nevertheless, Felix felt great anxiety for his kind commander and teacher. When Columbus slept, he mounted guard at the cabin door, crossbow in hand and Perrito by his side. And at night when the Admiral was on deck watching, or taking observations, Felix and his crossbow were close at hand to resist any act of treachery.

One eventful night, as Columbus was standing on the high stern of the *Santa Maria*, he suddenly started and uttered an exclamation. Glancing around, he saw Felix near by.

"Felix," he said quietly, "come here and tell me if thou seest anything in that direction."

Felix approached, and looked intently in the direction indicated. Presently he said:

"Señor, I see a light a long way off moving up and down."

THE NEW WORLD.

"Then I am not deceived," cried Columbus. "I have discovered LAND!"

He called two of his officers, and they too saw the distant light.

The night wore on, and every man in the fleet was wide awake and on the alert. At two o'clock in the morning a red flash lighted up the swelling sails of the *Pinta*,  and the report of a cannon electrified the expectant mariners. Following the report there came over the dark water a long-drawn, exultant cry, —

"*Land! land!*"

It was October 12, 1492.

In the fresh and lovely dawn Felix stood by the side of Columbus and gazed on the gleaming shore of a beautiful island. The pure, sweet air, the clear, azure sky, the pellucid waters, the green, luxuriant land, all filled the hearts of the voyagers with gladness, and seemed, indeed, to belong to a new and delightful world.

Had Ignacio Diaz been present, his heart would have swelled with pride to see the Admiral enter his boat attired in that rich suit of scarlet cloth embroidered with gold; and, doubtless, his chief reflection would have been of the numerous orders likely to be received from Don Christopher Columbus now that he had discovered a new world.

Well, poor Ignacio Diaz has been forgotten for centuries. I doubt that it ever occurred to him that anything but money was worth working for. If it had been suggested to him, he would have asked, with contempt, "Where is the profit coming in, Señor?" But a few years passed, and he died, and ducats were useless to him forever.

The boats touched the land, and Columbus stepped ashore with the royal standard in his hand. Felix followed him. Perrito had been left on the ship, and his mournful bay could be heard over the water. The officers and sailors landed. Down they all knelt upon the shore to thank God for success.

Then Columbus took possession of the

THE NEW WORLD. 141

land for the king and queen of Spain, whose admiral and viceroy he also proclaimed himself to be. And from the woods there came a crowd of wild, copper-

colored men to greet the strangers who had landed on their soil, — the soil that was to be theirs no more.

Columbus and his men remained on shore

the rest of the day, exploring the beautiful island, which the natives called Guanahani, and endeavoring to converse with the gentle though barbaric inhabitants. With presents of beads and hawk-bells they won the hearts of the simple people, and sought to learn from them more of the new world that they had found.

During the afternoon, Felix, attracted by the beauty of the woods, wandered away from his companions and strolled with delight among fragrant thickets, and under the broad, drooping leaves of tropic trees. He carried his crossbow in his hand, but he felt no fear of the natives.

After crossing a wooded point, and becoming somewhat entangled in dense underbrush, he at length emerged upon the beach. The surf broke gently on the white sand.

A cool breeze tempered the ardent rays of the sun. Over the blue water he saw the ships riding at anchor.

While he felt all the beauty of the scene, yet his mind was occupied with other thoughts. He realized that Columbus had achieved a great triumph. Well, so had he, Felix Madrigal, achieved a great triumph. Columbus had conquered the perils of a vast and unknown ocean, and had found a new world. What had Felix Madrigal conquered? *The alphabet!* Was not that a new world, too, surrounded likewise with strange and perplexing rocks and shoals whereon he had many times nearly suffered shipwreck? He sat down upon the sand, and with a twig began carefully to trace the letters of his name.

Suddenly his attention was drawn from his absorbing task. A strange object was emerging from the surf. Felix had often heard of mermaids and mermen, and he felt that something of that sort was now before his eyes. He laid his hand on his crossbow, though much doubting whether an arrow would prevail against a being of that kind.

As the creature emerged from the surf and crawled upon the beach, Felix was struck by an impression that he had seen something like it before. Still mystified, however, he remained motionless, and watched the singular movements of the newcomer, who began eagerly to pluck up handfuls of sand and hold it up to the sunlight and examine it intently.

Soon a young Indian came running swiftly along the beach. He was naked, and his long black hair streamed behind him as he sped along. In his hands he held a large ball of cotton. He had probably heard of the arrival of the strange white men, and was hastening to see them, with his ball of cotton for an offering.

As he drew near, the uncouth being on the sand reared itself to its feet right in his path. It was a disgusting revelation to Felix. He knew too well that brutal face, and those huge, projecting ears. It was the *contrabandista*. He had left the ship without permission and swum ashore, and was now vigorously prospecting for those marvellous sands of gold.

The Indian halted and gazed at him with evident fear. Then he tremblingly held out his ball of cotton, — his little offering that he had brought for the godlike visitors.

The *contrabandista* strode forward, with hand extended, also, but extended to take, not to give. That was his usual practice. But at that moment something about the savage seemed to inspire him with extreme emotion. He rushed forward and caught the unfortunate red man by the nose.

Felix heard the Indian cry out with pain, and realized that violence was being done. He snatched up his crossbow, placed an arrow on the string, and hurried forward, calling out sharply to the ruffian to desist.

The *contrabandista* turned upon him with a ferocious scowl, but perceiving the crossbow levelled at him, he began to parley and to make excuses. He confessed to swimming ashore, being urged to the act by his intense desire to touch land once more. He was merely protecting himself from the Indian, who he feared was about to attack him. He trusted that Felix would not report such a harmless escapade, and craved permission to swim back to the ship.

Felix felt that it was his duty to conduct the offender before Columbus, yet he disliked to get any one into trouble. He looked at the Indian and saw that he wore a small ornament of gold in his nose. It was this that the *contrabandista* had coveted and had endeavored to tear away. The blood was trickling down the poor fellow's face, and he seemed trembling between flying for his life and throwing himself at the feet of the white strangers.

Felix's indignation blazed up, and he wheeled about to command the ruffian to accompany him immediately to the Admiral. But the fellow had slipped away and was already in the surf striking out swiftly for the *Santa Maria*.

So Felix turned his attention to soothing the fears of the Indian, and after a time succeeded in assuring him of his friendship. His next effort was to ascertain his companion's name. Pointing to himself, he pronounced his own name, "Felix." Then pointing to the native he fixed upon him a look of inquiry. In a moment the Indian seemed to understand the question, and replied,—

"Poalo."

So Felix called him "Pablo," which had a similar sound, and presently conducted him to Columbus, to whom he reported also the cruel assault perpetrated by the *contrabandista*.

Pablo, perceiving that he was in the presence of the commander of the strange visitors, humbly offered his ball of cotton. Columbus accepted it with benignity, and gave him in return a red cap and a string of glass beads.

Joyful at receiving such rich and wonderful gifts, Pablo forgot his injured nose and fell to dancing on the greensward. Columbus meanwhile addressed his men, proclaiming dire penalties against whomsoever should maltreat the natives.

Nevertheless, every one present had marked with eager eyes and quickened breath the little ornament of gold in Pablo's nose, and when the Indian had finished his childish dance, Columbus sought to learn from him where he had obtained it. Pablo pointed to the south, and by signs and gestures and strange antics seemed to describe a great and rich monarch whose empire lay in that direction.

The Spaniards were exultant and joyful. They seemed to see just before them the gorgeous realization of their hopes. Their own ardent desire for the discovery of lands of enormous wealth guided them too closely in interpreting the fantastic sign language of the Indians.

"Gentlemen," said Columbus, "our course lies to the south. Doubtless the great monarch described by this Indian is that same king of the island of Cipango, or Japan, described by Marco Polo."

As night came on they all returned to the ships. The *contrabandista* was at once called to account for his misdeeds. He was put in chains, and assigned a diet of bread and water. The question of cutting off one of his ears was also seriously considered. But in view of the general joy prevailing in the fleet, this infliction was postponed for a time. Still, the ruffian was

THE NEW WORLD.

in a sad state, — his only ray of hope being the remembrance of that rude hoop of gold hanging from the Indian's nose.

Two days after, the fleet sailed southward from Guanahani, which Columbus called San Salvador. Seven Indians were taken on board the ships, to be taught the Spanish language, so that they could serve as interpreters. Among them was Pablo, who had become much attached to Felix, and begged to be taken with him. He was certainly the brightest of the seven, — gentle, affectionate, and obliging. Felix soon taught him to speak a little Spanish, and rewarded his efforts with biscuits and honey.

After touching at several beautiful islands, and seeking in vain for rich kingdoms, and mines of gold and gems, Columbus set sail for a great island to the south, which he fully believed to be the gorgeous Cipango of which he had long dreamed.

On the morning of the twenty-eighth of October there burst upon his view a grand and far-extending island, with lofty mountains, green plains and valleys, and vast forests. Clear and sparkling rivers flowed gently into the blue and tranquil sea. The beautiful wooded shores were fragrant with flowers and fruit. Birds of brilliant plumage flitted among the trees, and glittering insects flashed amongst the luxuriant verdure. It was Cuba, the "Queen of the Antilles."

The fleet coasted along these delightful

shores, and succeeded in opening communication with the inhabitants, but they were merely naked Indians, and brought little besides cotton to barter. There was no gold.

Again Columbus eagerly listened to the half-understood tales of the natives. They seemed to tell of a great king who dwelt at his magnificent capital in the interior of the island. Surely this must be some mighty Asiatic potentate. Columbus resolved to

THE NEW WORLD. 151

send envoys to communicate with the monarch.

Two men were chosen for this service, one of whom could speak Hebrew, Chaldaic, and Arabic. With Pablo and a Cuban Indian for interpreters, they set out on their adventurous journey, and disappeared in the dense forest.

The next day Felix accompanied Columbus on an expedition up the large river in the mouth of which the fleet was anchored. When the party landed to explore the adjacent country, they were attracted by a group of Indian huts in a beautiful grove not far away, and went to visit them.

They were built of palm leaves, and were quite clean. A goodly quantity of cotton and cotton yarn was stored within, and several hammocks of cotton net were suspended between posts.

Near the huts were small fields of cotton and Indian corn, and between the hills of corn were low, dark-green plants, each plant having a number of queer, roundish roots or tubers. Felix put a few of these roots in his pocket as curiosities. He tasted one of them, but at once concluded that it was not yet ripe.

After hanging a few beads on the huts,

to conciliate the owners, who had been seen hovering at a distance, the party returned to the boats.

In a few days the two envoys returned. They had been disappointed. The splendid city and the mighty king had shrunk into a cluster of Indian huts and a barbarian chief. Thus the cloud-castles crumbled.

Hearing from the natives accounts of an island of fabulous richness to the northeast, Columbus determined to sail thither. But soon after leaving the coast of Cuba, he was met by adverse winds, and compelled to put back.

The *Pinta*, having better sailing qualities, continued on her course, in spite of the Admiral's signals to return, and was soon lost to sight. Columbus was much troubled by this, as he believed it to be a deliberate desertion on the part of Martin Alonzo Pinzon, with the hope of securing more glory and profit to himself and to his townsmen and friends who were with him.

During this rough weather, the *contrabandista* was released from his chains and returned to duty, with both ears intact. So far from being grateful for this, he soon gathered a few of his familiar spirits about him in the forecastle, and over a tankard of wine mumbled ferocious threats against Columbus and Felix. But the ruffian attended to his duties promptly, and no one suspected the plot that was forming in his evil mind, — a plot that was destined to bring disaster.

When the weather became more favorable, the *Santa Maria* and the *Niña* again sailed to the east, and soon the island of Hayti loomed grandly above the horizon. As they approached, the mariners were delighted by the almost magical beauty of that tropic isle of the sea.

It was a populous land, but the natives fled at the approach of the ships. But at last some of the sailors captured an Indian girl. She was taken on board the *Santa Maria*, and kindly treated, and released with many presents. Again the hearts of the Spaniards beat high with hope, for the girl wore an ornament of gold in her nose.

The kind treatment of the girl had the intended effect, and the explorers were soon surrounded by thousands of gentle and generous natives. Little gold was found, but they heard wondrous tales of rich mines farther on. So they continued their voyage along the northern coast.

On the twenty-second of December, a large canoe full of Indians came alongside of the *Santa Maria* bringing a native dignitary. He announced himself a messenger from the great cacique, Guacanagari, at whose dominions the ships had now arrived. He brought as a present to the Admiral a belt of wampum, and a carved mask of wood and gold. He bore, also, an invitation to Columbus to visit the cacique at his royal residence a little farther along the coast.

Columbus accepted the invitation. Aside from the strange desertion of Pinzon, fortune seemed about to favor the expedition. They had at last reached the dominions of a powerful cacique. Gold was becoming plentiful among the natives, and they willingly parted with it. But, above all, marvellous tales were told of a king in the mountains of the interior whose wealth was boundless, and whose very banners were of gold. His realm was called Cibao, and Columbus, catching at the similarity of the names, was assured that at last he had reached Cipango.

On Christmas eve, 1492, the *Santa Maria* and the *Niña* were sailing along the coast toward the capital of the cacique, Guacanagari. The night was calm, the sea was smooth, and no danger seemed possible.

Late at night Columbus retired to his cabin. The officer of the deck, trusting in the quiet night, also went below. The helmsman, feeling drowsy, presently called one of the ship-boys to take the tiller, and he, too, lay down to sleep. The boy nodded at his post.

Perrito was lying at the cabin door as usual, while Felix had wrapped himself in his cloak and was asleep on the lee side of the deck, as was his custom on pleasant nights.

A man crept stealthily from the forecastle and stole aft in the deepest shadows. He paused amidships and bent down to examine a sleeping figure on the deck. It was Felix, with his crossbow beside him. The man shook his fist at the unconscious boy, but did not then disturb him. He turned away and approached the drowsy lad at the helm.

"Here, boy, sleep awhile. I'll steer," he whispered hoarsely. The lad looked up and recognized the *contrabandista*. But he was very willing to be relieved. He gave up the tiller and was soon snoring on the deck.

The *contrabandista* did some singular steering. It was not long before he heard the dull roar of breakers, and saw them flashing white in the gloom dead ahead. His wicked eyes glared like those of a cat in the dark.

Suddenly he stepped forward and kicked the sleeping ship-boy.

"Get up and take the helm, you young cub; it's my turn to snooze," he growled.

The boy, startled out of a sound sleep, rose, half awake, and took the tiller. The *contrabandista* hurried forward in the darkness. Bending over Felix, who still lay in a profound slumber, he suddenly lifted him and flung him over the rail into the sea. Then he darted forward into the forecastle.

A moment after, the ship struck heavily and trembled, from bow to stern. The breakers roared hoarsely around her. The affrighted boy at the helm screamed an alarm. Then the deck was crowded with the dark figures of the terrified crew. They rushed about in a wild panic. Frenzied shouts and orders mingled in the dreadful tumult. Again the sea raised the doomed ship, and again she crashed on the sands.

CHAPTER VIII.

THE RETURN TO SPAIN.

It was a sudden and disagreeable awakening for Felix, to find himself tossing among the breakers. He was entangled in his cloak, and in imminent danger of drowning. But just as he began to grow faint with exhaustion, he felt himself seized and supported, and realized that his rescuer was drawing him away from the breakers into smoother water.

He was half strangled with salt water, and coughed and gasped so desperately that it was some minutes before he could endeavor to ascertain who the strong swimmer was that had saved his life. As he recovered, he tried to strike out for himself, but his companion did not release his firm grasp on his jacket.

They were moving slowly through the water.

"Who are you, *amigo?*" asked Felix, at last, when he felt that he could spare a little breath.

"Pablo," replied a gentle, well-known voice at his ear.

"Pablo!" cried Felix, with a burst of gratitude, "you have saved my life!"

They swam on. Distant shouts and cries came to their ears. Felix did not realize their meaning. He did not know that the ship had gone ashore. He was still bewildered. Around him was a vast waste of waters amid which he was lost. He knew not where he was nor whither he was going. Had he been alone, terror and despair would have seized him.

"Where are we going?" he asked, presently.

"Going ashore," replied Pablo calmly.

They swam on and on. Felix's heart began to sink. He was becoming exhausted. Could they ever reach the land?

Pablo marked his weakening strokes and his sobbing breath. His grasp tightened a little.

"Rest, Felix, rest," he said gently.

In a short time Felix was compelled to rest. Had he been alone, he must have sunk like a stone. But his companion bore him steadily on.

At last, a dull roar sounded in his ears. He saw phosphorescent lights flickering along the crest of the breaking surf. He felt the strong waves carrying them in.

And then Pablo was bearing him through the shallow water, and laying him down upon the white sand.

Felix lay for a little while in a sort of stupor, while Pablo watched anxiously beside him. When he had recovered a little strength, he questioned the Indian as to the nature of the accident that had befallen him.

Pablo described in vivid pantomime, and

with what words he could command, the dastardly deed of the *contrabandista*. The Indian had been asleep on the forecastle, but being awakened by the noise of the breakers, he had sprung up just in time to witness the cowardly act and to leap overboard to the assistance of Felix. He had not recognized the perpetrator of the deed, but Felix was convinced that there was but one man on board the *Santa Maria* who could have done it.

Felix was thunderstruck when Pablo asserted that the ship had gone ashore in the breakers. He could hardly believe it, but his mind was filled with dismal forebodings of a dire calamity. It was not for a long time that the probability of his own private loss occurred to him. But then it pierced him like an arrow, and a sorrowful cry burst from his lips.

"My crossbow! It is lost!"

Pablo heard and understood, but said nothing. They sat on the beach drearily waiting for morning to dawn. Felix remembered that it was Christmas day, and was about to mention it to Pablo, when it occurred to him that Pablo was a heathen, and he felt deep pity at the thought.

But Felix himself had few pleasant recollections connected with the holiday. The only Christmas he had ever spent that could be called "merry" was the one he had passed in Lisbon, and that was very merry indeed. Little did he then dream that in a year he would be sitting on the vast shore of a new world, with a wild Indian for a companion.

The weather was mild, so that in spite of his drenched clothing, Felix did not suffer. As for Pablo, the water vanished from his copper skin like quicksilver.

The night wore on. Felix fell asleep and dreamed that he was again in Vascoña's splendid house at Lisbon. The brilliant halls were crowded with Christmas revellers, and he heard music, and laughter, and the rhythmic tap of dancing feet. Suddenly he awoke and started up. The glorious dawn was breaking. Pablo sat silent beside him. He held the crossbow in his hand.

"Pablo!" cried Felix, "where did you find my crossbow?"

"Ship," replied Pablo, with a wave of his hand seaward.

Felix looked, and, with a sharp pang of grief, saw the *Santa Maria* a long way out, dismantled and lying on her side on a sand bar, with the waves breaking against her.

"Was the crossbow on the ship?"

"Yes."

"How did you get it?"

"Swim," replied Pablo gently.

"Is there any one on the ship?"

"No. All gone. *Niña*," answered Pablo.

"Good boy, Pablo!" cried Felix, seizing his crossbow with one hand, and slapping his companion on the back with the other. "You've saved my crossbow and me. If there are any biscuits and honey left on the *Niña*, you'll get them — all you can eat!"

Pablo smiled joyously.

In a little while a boat was seen approaching from the *Niña*. It soon reached the shore, and two men landed. Felix and Pablo hastened to meet them. They proved to be Diego de Arana, the judge of the fleet, and Pedro Gutierrez. the king's butler. They stared at Felix with astonishment.

"Art thou a ghost?" said Arana. "We had all given thee up for dead. The Admiral is sorely grieved."

"How did you get ashore?" asked Gutierrez.

"I fell into the sea, and Pablo saved my life and brought me ashore," replied Felix.

"Ah," said Arana dubiously, "I doubt the virtue of having one's life saved by a heathen. Methinks it were better to sink. Yes, that would be my decision. It were better to sink."

"Señor," returned Felix gravely, "before making your decision, pray allow yourself to be taken while asleep and thrown into the sea at the dead of night. Methinks you will find even the assistance of a heathen acceptable."

"How!" cried Arana, in astonishment. "Were you thrown into the sea?"

"Yes, Señor."

"Who committed such a heinous crime?"

"My suspicions lack proof, Señor."

"This shall be investigated. I, too, have

suspicions. Let the guilty man beware should I secure proof, also. We are going to the cacique, Guacanagari, to inform him of the disaster. You may accompany us if you wish. This Indian, though a heathen, may be useful as an interpreter."

After a brisk walk, they reached the capital town of the cacique, built among lovely groves. Their approach had been observed, and Guacanagari himself came forth to meet them, surrounded by many of his officers. He was a man of frank and ingenuous countenance, and majestic yet gentle manners. He was attired in a cotton robe, and wore on his head a heavy coronet of gold from which arose brilliant plumes of parrot's feathers.

His delight at meeting the white men was changed to genuine sorrow when he learned of the disaster to the *Santa Maria*. The tears rolled down his cheeks as he tried to express his grief.

He turned and gave orders to his officers, and soon a thousand Indians were hurrying to the beach and embarking in canoes to go to the assistance of Columbus.

THE RETURN TO SPAIN. 167

Felix and Pablo accompanied Arana and Gutierrez on board the *Niña*, and the Admiral received Felix with a joy that testified how deep had been his sorrow at his supposed loss.

The cacique soon followed to sympathize with and comfort Columbus, and to oversee

the work of unloading the wreck. So faithfully did the Indians prosecute the work, that in a short time the cargo and arms and stores were landed. And so great was the honesty of these heathen, whom Arana scorned, that nothing was misappropriated or stolen.

A day or two afterward, Columbus visited the cacique at his town, accompanied by a large number of his officers and men. Felix and Pablo were with the party. After a dinner at the house of Guacanagari, the visitors witnessed a great celebration in a neighboring grove, where a thousand Indians danced to the music of drums and castanets while they chanted wild native songs.

Columbus returned this peaceful entertainment by displaying the warlike skill of his men with crossbow, sword, and arquebuse. Felix was called forth and shot arrows into a tree at a great distance, to the wonder and admiration of the Indians. Finally one of the cannon of the *Santa Maria* that had been brought ashore was fired, and the stunning report changed the wonder of the natives to terror.

Columbus now resolved to build a fort near the town of the friendly Guacanagari, and leave a colony there. The wreck of the *Santa Maria* was broken up and the timbers brought ashore to be used in constructing the fortress.

The sailors worked with a will, for many of them were anxious to remain on the island where gold seemed to be plentiful, and where they could lead indolent lives, quite different from their existence on board ship.

There was one miserable man on the *Niña* whose fierce passions were excited by the tidings of this proposed colony. It was the *contrabandista*. He had again been put in chains at the instance of Arana, who suspected him of throwing Felix overboard, although he had as yet no proof. The ship-boy had not dared to tell what he knew. The *contrabandista* knew that it was idle for him to hope to be left as one of the colonists, yet that was what he ardently desired. So he raged in his chains like a wild beast. The knowledge that Felix had escaped, increased his fury.

In a short time the fort was finished, and cannon mounted for its defence. Thirty-nine men were chosen to remain as colonists, and were solemnly charged to treat the Indians with kindness and justice, and to collect all the gold they could. Perhaps all this was too much to expect of ordinary mortals. At any rate, they seem to have made a dismal failure of it.

When all was ready, Columbus took affectionate leave of the friendly cacique and his generous people, and of the comrades he was about to leave behind, and the *Niña* set sail and departed.

Hardly had she got well to sea, when the *contrabandista's* chains were found, but they no longer held that ruffian in their cold embrace. He had been liberated by some confederate, and had swum ashore to join the colony.

He jumped from the frying-pan into the fire, for the officer left in command of the colony was Diego de Arana himself. If that severe judge failed to hang him at once, the *contrabandista* certainly shared the fate of the whole party, for before Columbus's return, every man was massacred. By their own wicked conduct they had brought upon themselves the just vengeance of the Indians.

As the *Niña* was bounding along with all sails set, Felix came upon Pablo seated upon a coil of rope in an attitude of deep dejection, and gazing mournfully over the blue water.

"What is the matter, Pablo?" he asked.

"Guanahani," murmured Pablo, looking up.

"Oh, your island, — your home?"

"Yes, Guanahani."

"What about it? Do you want to go back there?"

"Yes, — go back," said Pablo eagerly.

"What! Are you homesick?"

"Want Guanahani," was the plaintive reply.

"But we're going to Spain, now, — to my country. It's the greatest country in the world. You'll see great things. Perhaps you'll see the king and queen, — and so will I," cried Felix, swelling with importance at the thought.

"Guanahani," sighed poor Pablo.

"But we'll come back again, you know," continued Felix. "Then you can see Guanahani, Pablo."

When he comprehended that idea, Pablo brightened perceptibly, and Felix made haste further to comfort him with biscuits and honey.

Two days after leaving the colony, they fell in with the *Pinta*. In spite of the inexcusable desertion of her commander, it was a joyful meeting, and the two ships prepared for the long voyage back to Spain. Pinzon had achieved nothing more glorious than cruising along the coast and trading with the Indians.

In a few days they entered a deep inlet of the sea on the island of Hayti. Here the Spaniards found a fierce and warlike tribe of Indians armed with bows and arrows, war-clubs, and javelins.

It was at this place that Felix performed a feat that made him famous among the sailors. He accompanied a party of well-armed men who were sent ashore to trade with the savages. They were met by a large band of Indians fully armed and hideously painted. While the sailors were endeavoring to purchase some of their bows and arrows, the Indians seemed to become suspicious and threatened an attack. The Spaniards instantly set upon them, wounded two, and put the rest to flight.

Felix at the time had his crossbow in hand, and was trying to purchase a bow from a gigantic savage of ferocious aspect. The trade seemed difficult, as the Indian persisted in demanding the crossbow in exchange.

When the hostile demonstration was made, the huge savage snatched the crossbow from Felix and made off with it at a swift pace. The other Indians were already running through the woods, and the commander of the Spaniards checked the pursuit of his men and drew them back to the boat. All obeyed but Felix, who ran fiercely on far into the forest in pursuit of the savage who had taken his crossbow. In vain his comrades shouted to him to return.

The big Indian ran for some distance and then halted among the dense thickets to admire his prize. While he was thus pleasantly engaged, Felix burst upon him furiously and snatched the weapon from his hands, with loud and angry words.

The red giant looked down upon the slender white boy with amazement, and then burst into a loud laugh, while Felix promptly retreated, and soon met his companions hastily advancing to his rescue.

The next day the Indians returned in great numbers. But they exhibited a very friendly spirit, and their chief gave Columbus the wampum belt of peace, and his own coronet of gold.

Soon afterward the ships set sail for Spain. The return voyage was very severe. Dreadful storms arose, and for many days they were scourged by fierce winds, and tossed upon gigantic billows, in imminent danger of shipwreck.

The poor Indians whom Columbus was taking to Spain were terrified beyond measure. Several of them fell sick. Among these was poor Pablo. Felix remained beside him almost constantly, striving to alleviate his distress. But the poor Indian was like a plant plucked from its native soil and slowly withering. He forgot the strange words that he had learned from Felix. He turned away from the biscuits and sweet honey that he had liked so well. They could not tempt him now. He lay with mournful, piteous eyes, and the only moan that broke from his lips was the name, "Guanahani."

One dreadful night of howling storm, Felix sat beside Pablo, holding his thin hand and sadly watching his face as the dim lamp swung to and fro. Suddenly the Indian started and sat up. His head was bent eagerly forward. A look of intense delight came over his face. His eyes were bright and glad; they seemed to be gazing on scenes far away.

"*Guanahani!*" he cried joyfully.

Then his muscles relaxed,— the light faded from his eyes,— he fell back dead.

Soon the rude sailors came and bore away the body, and threw it into the roaring sea. It was a sad fate for the poor barbarian, torn from his peaceful island, and Felix shed many tears for him. Yet it was better than that of thousands of his unfortunate countrymen who afterward wore out their lives in hopeless slavery.

Storm after storm shattered the unhappy

ships. The *Pinta* disappeared in the tempest, and it was feared that she had sunk. Columbus, fearing that any day might see the *Niña* engulfed in the depths of the angry ocean, wrote an account of his discoveries, enclosed it in a barrel, and threw it into the sea, so that if his ships were lost, the world might yet hear the result of his voyage.

After stopping at one of the Azores, and being very treacherously treated by the Portuguese governor, who had received orders to detain Columbus should he touch there, the *Niña* again set sail.

And again furious storms assailed the weather-beaten ship. At last, sighting land at the mouth of the Tagus on the fourth of March, they were forced to run in for shelter, into the lion's mouth, as it were.

The news of Columbus's arrival and of his great discovery soon spread, and many distinguished visitors came on board the *Niña* to hear accounts of the voyage and see the strange copper-colored men from the Indies.

Felix was now among familiar scenes,

THE RETURN TO SPAIN.

and he often thought of Vascoña. He watched, a little apprehensively, each boat that arrived, fearing lest the cavalier might take advantage of their feeble condition to commit some act of revenge. But Vascoña did not appear.

In a few days a dignitary arrived bearing an invitation from the king of Portugal for Columbus to visit him at Court. Although Columbus distrusted the king, yet he deemed it best to accept the invitation. Several of his officers were to accompany him, and Columbus kindly gave Felix permission to go. For once Felix would have preferred to remain on board the ship, but, fearing to be thought cowardly, he said nothing, and went with the party.

Everything needed for their journey was magnificently provided, and they soon arrived at Court. The king received them graciously, and entertained them with fine hospitality. Columbus described his voyage, and though the king's envy and mortification were evident, yet he listened with intense interest and close attention.

One day, as Felix was at an assembly in

one of the halls of the palace, a hand was laid on his shoulder. He turned, and saw Vascoña. The cavalier looked very grave.

"Felix," he said, "I did not think to see thee here. Didst thou accompany Columbus on his voyage?"

"Yes, Señor."

"Where didst thou join him?"

"At the island of Gomera."

"I heard of thee there. Didst thou warn him of my expedition?"

"Yes, Señor."

"I admire thy candor and courage," said Vascoña. "But didst thou not act treacherously? Is that the way thou repayest one who saved thy life?"

"I remember all your kindness," replied Felix. "But saving my life did not make me your slave. I am still free to serve my friends and my country."

"Let it pass," said Vascoña, smiling. "I was only trying thee. I hold thee under no obligations for running away with thee. I well believe that thou wouldst sooner lose thy life than thy freedom. But now that thou hast finished thy voyage, wilt thou not come to live with me again? Everything thou mayst wish for shall be thine. Stay with me, Felix."

"I thank you very much, Señor," replied Felix gently. "But I would rather serve my own country."

Vascoña now led him to a private apartment, and asked him many questions about the voyage, which Felix answered as well as he could. At last the cavalier said, seriously, —

"Felix, I esteem thee highly, and I will give thee a warning concerning thy master. Bid him leave this Court as soon as possible. Warn him to engage in no controversy with any one here. There is a despicable plot among some of the jealous courtiers to assassinate him, and so, if possible, rob him of his well-earned honors."

Felix was greatly startled by this, and when he had left Vascoña he lost no time in warning Columbus.

The next day they left the Court, with great honors, and returned to the ship. Nothing more was heard of the plot of assassination, but it was afterward discovered that Vascoña had reason for the warning he gave. Such a plot really existed.

On the thirteenth of March the *Niña* again put to sea, and on the fifteenth, about noon, entered the harbor of Palos in triumph.

The reception of Columbus and his men may be imagined, — how the bells rung out a joyful peal, and the excited multitude hurried to the landing to greet the daring mariners, returned from an unknown bourne as from the dead.

In the evening the joy was made complete by the arrival of the *Pinta*, which had been driven north by the storm into the bay of Biscay.

When Felix landed with Columbus, the first persons they met were Father Juan Perez, the physician, Garcia Fernandez, Tortosa, and Diego, who was visiting La Rabida. There was a most joyful greeting.

"Welcome, Felix!" cried Diego, throwing his arms about his friend. "Has my father found heaven, and brought you back?"

"Felix! I never thought to see thee again," cried Tortosa, the tears running down his wrinkled face.

"Perrito! good Perrito!" laughed Diego, as the faithful dog leaped upon him. "I told thee to find Felix, and thou hast done thy duty, old fellow!"

At that moment another familiar voice was heard, and the physician, Garcia Fernandez, took Felix by the shoulder.

"Well, young man, have you just got back? I shall be careful next time whom I send to La Rabida with a letter, promising to pay for his time till he comes back. Never mind, you've been well employed, I hear. I have just paid Ignacio Diaz for three months of your time. He has not pined away grieving for you, Felix. We'll make another arrangement, I think. I do not believe you were born to be a tailor." And the good doctor laughed and grew red in the face.

"Felix! my dear Felix!" cried a husky voice, and Ignacio Diaz himself shambled out of the noisy crowd and tried to embrace his apprentice. "Thou hast been to the

Indies, they say. Tell me, hast thou thy pockets full of precious stones? Is the ship laden with gold?" And the tailor's eyes bulged out eagerly.

Felix laughed, and thrust his hands in his pockets, which were full of odd curiosities. He drew out a small object. It was one of the curious roots that he had found in Cuba.

"Here is something I picked up in the Indies," he said, and held it out to Ignacio Diaz. The tailor snatched it hastily. It was merely a roundish root or tuber, with a smooth skin in which were numerous slight indentations. He gazed at it a moment, touched it with his tongue and rubbed it on his sleeve, and then threw it down angrily.

Tortosa picked it up, and it was examined curiously, while they all laughed at the tailor's disappointment. But none of them knew that it was really a great treasure, — the humble *potato*.

Felix and Diego accompanied Columbus to Barcelona, where the sovereigns gave the discoverer of the New World a truly royal reception as "Admiral of the Ocean sea, and Viceroy and Governor of the islands discovered in the Indies."

Felix remained in the service of Columbus until the latter's death. He became an honored companion of Diego when he succeeded to his father's honors.

In 1519, he was one of the most trusted captains of Cortez in his invasion of Mexico, and fought in many of the battles of the Conquest.

He remained in the New World that he had helped to discover and conquer, holding positions of high honor, and distinguished above his military compeers for justice and mercy. He died in the City of Mexico, aged seventy years.

www.ingramcontent.com/pod-product-compliance
Lightning Source LLC
Chambersburg PA
CBHW020847160426
43192CB00007B/824